New Selected Poems

ROBERT MINHINNICK was born in 1952 and lives in south Wales. He has published nine collections of poetry, including *The Adulterer's Tongue*, translations of works by six Welsh poets. He has been the winner of a Society of Authors Eric Gregory Award and a Cholmondeley Award, and has twice won the Forward Prize for best individual poem. His books of essays have twice won the Wales Book of the Year Prize. His first novel, *Sea Holly*, was published by Seren in 2007. Robert Minhinnick edited *Poetry Wales* magazine from 1997 to 2008. He co-founded Friends of the Earth (Cymru) and Sustainable Wales, and is an advisor to Sustainable Wales.

T0290158

Also by Robert Minhinnick from Carcanet Press

Selected Poems
After the Hurricane
King Driftwood

As editor and translator
The Adulterer's Tongue: Six Welsh Poets

ROBERT MINHINNICK

New Selected Poems

CARCANET

First published in Great Britain in 2012 by

Carcanet Press Limited
Alliance House
Cross Street
Manchester M2 7AQ

www.carcanet.co.uk

The publisher acknowledges financial assistance from Arts Council England

Supported by
ARTS COUNCIL
ENGLAND

Typeset by XL Publishing Services, Tiverton
Printed and bound in England by SRP Ltd, Exeter

Contents

from
A Thread in the Maze
1978

Sap

Where the stream ox-bowed
And we stood on a bulwark
Of planks and turf, the current
Made its darkest passage,
A black stillwater, treacherous
Beneath a sheen of scum.

Once, and only once, a trout rose,
Its lean sides gleaming like
A knife between the stones,
Crimson shadow at its belly.
Yet how often was the only sound
Not the Ffornwg or our
White thrash after fish,
But the thinnest flute of the sap
Maintaining its single note
A long minute in my head
As I imagined that pressure
Of water rising through the trees,
Streams moving vertically
And spilling in a silent turbulence
Along the boughs, a river

Flowing there beneath the bark,
The sap, singing, even as flesh
Leaned white and stunned
Against the visible current,
And the gwrachen like a small
Green stick swam past the hand.

Short Wave

I try to tune in, but Europe's blurred voice
Becomes stranger with the movement of the dial.

All stations seem to give a fragment of
Performance – Mozart disarmed by a fizzled
Prodigy: innumerable cliques of wordsmiths.

As the electric crackles I make believe
I am composing an avant-garde symphony,
A sound poem for a hall of idiot speech.

But behind the static are moments of sanity;
A string quartet and interesting chanteuse,
Then histrionics at a play's climax.

For some reason, a hubbub of languages
And dim music becomes more important
Than any scheduled programme. It suits

My mood perhaps, this indecipherable mayhem
Of newscasters and sopranos, and the long
Returns to electronic gibbering.

Somewhere, behind a rock band's sudden squall,
A Morse message is tapped out. For a few seconds
It is clear, articulate, before melting

Into Europe's verbiage. It was not mayday.
And I twist the dial a hair's breadth into jazz.

A Live Tradition

1

Enamelled with idyllic scenes
The blue English china
Remained immaculately
Preserved in the *seld*

Whilst you ate out
Of newspaper, unshaven
In a vinegar-coloured suit,
Remembering in your storyteller's kitchen

A man arriving on foot
From Cirencester,
Stonemason with a mandolin
Inside a painted box,

And the farm, Tŷ Mawr,
Dazzled against the hill's
Bronze bulwark of light,
Its escarpment of quarrystone

Beneath scaffolding of briars,
The hissing swifts
Rebounding like boomerangs
From a high cornice.

2

You would be surprised
How often I think of this,
But the currency of your
Small legend still holds good,

If merely for
Its curiosity's sake.
In the not-quite-honest way of poetry
I acknowledge a debt,

For you were an anchor on the past
And the strong chain of your memory
Plummeted a sea
I wanted to explore,

And may have glimpsed,
When, emerging from a scrimmage
Of light and fowls,
I found you sleeping off a drunk

On the ridiculous
Wooden cask of the privy,
The gnats drawing white wires
Through your skull,

The grub-coloured flesh
Revealed beneath the parted rags,
Your spittle poised to fall
Like scorn's slow syllables.

3

But once I stood here
Exultant and afraid
Blowing a new luminosity
Into a swallow's egg,

Watching the sudden
Bubble of orange blood
Sliding into the dust;
And here, crouched to stroke

With frightened fingers
The slow worm's bronze glass,
Hardly able to comprehend
Such cold communion.

For this was the orchard
Of explosive experience;
The cavernous apples
Our sandals crushed to pulp,

Their militant grubs
Writhing in a fan of blossom,
Suspended on invisible threads
Above our opened mouths.

4

Now, in the kneeling light
Of ruined barns
I ponder your legacy
Of riddles,
           'gathering from the air
           a live tradition',

Yet knowing this inheritance
Is the rats' dark shoal of grain
Spilling from an attic
Cold, fungoid,

Brief as the sermon
Broadcast at the grave-slot,
The final despair
That scratched the mind's frail pane,

Sent you wandering
That freezing feast-night
Your own stiff fields
To the dirty manger,

The familiar
Bearlike shuffle
Of a shy man.

from *Herbals*

Garlic Mustard

Surprising with its
Cool fever of smells,
Each white boss of petals
Like the architecture of frost.

Fishscales of lichen
On the elder twigs,
The garlic stink
Oozing from beech-earth

As the herb's tap-root
Is pulled wriggling like a mole
Into sunlight,
Pale filament, root-fragment

Spread like the yellow
Human span of mole-hands.
Here amidst blonde ferns
Uncurling from their limestone sockets

And the cuckoo pint's
Alarming black phalli
Prepuced with dew,
This smooth and glossy nettle

Pours its own potency
Of odour into my fingertips,
Over my searching mouth,
Its acrid relish cauterising
All blander blossom.

Dawn: Cwrt y Felin

A pack of owls –
Herd of solitaries –
Continue lardering
The night's kill,
Their voices fanged
Medieval saws
Against the present's bone.

Again I have come
Unbidden to the cwrt
Where a smudge of fox
Eludes as it has always done
An agonised approach,
The man-abandoned court
Of rushes, yellow with

Goat willow, strewn by
Railway lunchwrappings,
Where an iron range,
Liverish with rust
Leaks straw and roaches'
Black hauberks,
To watch Nant Ffornwg

Like a mammal
Sinewed with light
Rushing ferociously
On the weir, then sliding
Flatly, eel-devious
Through the sluice,
The thin sleeve of the river

Pleated with foam,
Its dying drift of sallow
Gluing the stream-slot.
Surely in this flood

Two currents merge; my unbelief,
My violent need to praise,
Though pewter-coloured water

Paned with light, remains untouched
By such conventional devotion.
Here in the cwrt, a moment's
Affirmation fires the hogweed
And its hollow pipes, these empty tines
Once flower-fat, revealed in dead
Intricacies. I spin the spokes,
Shake out the iron seed.

1921: The Grandfather's Story

1976. Europe uniquely dry,
A vast blond savannah;
No end to such weather.
But the grandfather's tale
Concerned another year,
A striking, starved Glamorgan
The continent of his experience.

Ffornwg reduced to one
Green rope of water, glutinous
With gnats, and the village men
Moithered by heat, the latest scabs,
And an army of imported police
Billeted like Stuart troops.

Moonlight over a deserted
Countryside. Only the birds
Audible in air tarnished
By water's slow decay.
Boys scrabbling for coalcrumbs
In the forbidden pits. No rain three months.
Even Nant Iechyd rusty, dangerous.

But what he recalls tonight,
The grandfather amongst the bar's
Shirtsleeved crush, are the
Extraordinary voices of dying trout,
Like the mewling of newborn kittens,
Their shrill tumult shocking his mind

As he ladled fish from a shrinking pool,
Twenty-two thin and mottled bodies
Like half-opened jack-knives in the dry grass,
And only the eels, a villainous
Purple escaping, and the bells
Striking four as he walked home,
And the sun rising.

from
Native Ground
1979

Ways of Learning

We work together in the summer heat,
Each with his own method. I have
No facts, only the poem's approach
To knowledge, no memory but the glass
Of metaphor I hold like a mirror
To the past, crouching with a stub until
The marvellous telegraph flickers out.

But the old man has another way.
Pressing the seeds into the drills
I hear him talk of earlier gardens
Planted, harvested, and how these beans
Now red and black like chaffinch eggs
Will explode slowly through darkness,
Springing up in carrion fragrance

For the careful gardener. I see
His hard fists plunge again and again
Into the seed-pannier, the gravel
Of husks and their delicate kernels
Like ammunition in his hands,
A mystery still, unknowable,
But the bud of knowledge breaking in him.

The Children

Their squints and stammers disappeared,
The crooked teeth straightened somehow.
Difficult to tell if they need you now,
These fastidious young, your children,
Sipping glittering gin through their own ice.

Talk of experience, you're still the novice:
Already they have covered the world,
England, France, it's a motorway ride
In a friend's car, the music blasting
As they overtake your careful saloon.

Yet you still pretend to know these strangers,
Passing round photographs of children
They used to be, the horses ridden,
The mountains climbed. Look closer, you think,
And you will see yourself, a figure

In the background smiling at something
Out of the picture. Yet you will wonder
At your own permanence. Make supper then,
You're good at that, but already
They are waving goodbye through the frozen

Brilliance of windscreens, driving
To a life where their backs form a tight
Circle. Are you ever discussed?
There's never a silence in their intricate conversations;
And they forgot to mention when they are coming again.

J.P.

Trespassing, we were caught like moths
In the headlight trap of the Wolseley.
We glimpsed his face behind the windscreen,
The bright figurine on the car bonnet
Pointing at our guilt. In that world
He was legend, a tiny octogenarian
In panama and summer suit
Poised with secateurs above a rose-stem,
Or tapping with the polished ferrule
Of his cane through the gutter dust.

I remember the inquisitive gleam
Of his eyes, head cocked like a woodmouse,
As he regarded the extent of our crime,
Still the magistrate at the bench,
The jealous landowner. In the mansion-house
We had burgled rooms he never opened,
Broken the seal of the dust. And now,
Awaiting sentence, we shifted resentfully
In that hot stain of light. For Llangewydd's
Square mile of history, its cwms and
Slow decaying farms, the blaze of lawn about
The magistrate's estate, was an inheritance
We claimed. Even then the idea was alive
Within us: we belonged; we continued;
For ours was an instinct that mastered fear
And fired a tribal defiance of that
Black car as we stood our ground,
Staring together into its powerful beam.

Llangewydd

Sometimes at night for those who know
   Where to listen their signals run
Over the common like living telegraphs.

It seems their song is how evening
   Identifies itself, a masque that drifts
   From no distinct direction.
Eight o'clock on a spring night I came
   Quickly to a halt. The air was filled
   With the rattle of nightjars,
Their voices whirring like knives on a grindstone.

Not hard then to translate that sound
    As air grew cool and the slate-coloured light
    Thickened. As an invocation
Of time's hidden strata the nightjars
    Kept their medieval drone,
    No music in it, no relief,
Only the endless reel of things past,

Old hurts, some grief,
    And the life that persists like the stone
And has no one to speak for it.

The Drinking Art

    The altar of glasses behind the bar
Diminishes our talk. As if in church
The solitary men who come here
Slide to the edges of each black
Polished bench and stare at their hands.
    The landlord keeps his own counsel.

    This window shows a rose and anchor
Like a sailor's tattoo embellished
In stained glass, allows only the vaguest
Illumination of floor and ceiling,
The tawny froth the pumps sometimes spew.
    And the silence settles. The silence settles

    Like the yellow pinpoints of yeast
Falling through my beer, the bitter
That has built the redbrick
Into the faces of these few customers,
Lonely practitioners of the drinking art.
    Ashtrays, a slop-bucket, the fetid

Shed-urinal, all this I wondered at,
Running errands to the back-doors of pubs,
Woodbines and empty bottles in my hands.
Never become a drinking-man, my
Grandmother warned, remembering Merthyr
     And the Spanish foundry men

     Puking their guts up in the dirt streets,
The Irish running from the furnaces
To crowd their paymaster into a tavern,
Leather bags of sovereigns bouncing on his thigh.
But it is calmer here, more subtly dangerous.
     This afternoon is a suspension of life

     I learn to enjoy. But now
The towel goes over the taps and I feel
The dregs in my throat. A truce has ended
And the clocks start again. Sunlight
Leaps out of the street. In his shrine of glass
     The landlord is wringing our lives dry.

Insomnia

1

Whisky too a form of prayer.
Do not despise it.
At its red coal the night is warmed,
The hours come alive.

2

Lampshade, wardrobe, writing desk:
The shapes of life within this room
Float gently on the night's surface.

Aspirin and a hangover; blue line
Of water in my glass untouched;
Sunlight white as salt already

Stinging in the eye. Get up, move naked
Round and round a chair, the cactus
Trailing leaves across the sill,

Spilling its pale thorns on record sleeves:
Insomnia my curious disease,
First light and yet its dry fever still burns.

3

Tonight my wife sleeps evenly,
Her breath the convalescent
Murmur of waves we heard today
At Rhych, climbing as we did
In the high sea-dunes, exhausting
Ourselves in an ascent of that
Brief wilderness. Truly I belong
With her in sleep, but the sand
Has blown into my eyes
And I must stumble rough
And fully conscious, still

Following the ledges of Cwm-y-gaer,
A hillside brittle with
The ancient white deposits

Of snailshells, thick as the husks
On a threshing floor, so sharp
They pierce all defence,
Like these thorns in my eyes.

Sker

Everywhere the sea, pungent as mustard.
We come over the ploughland to the dunes
And realise this is all we know
Of wilderness – scarps rising like
Marram-green combers at the tide's
Fringe, their waves inching towards
The waves in the glacial progress of sand.

A hawk, a dunghill, the concrete foxholes
Made for war. Christ, the wind cuts,
It cuts right through. Before history
We are naked children not seeing
The storm, climbing over the rusted
Wire of the gun-range while the sea's
Artillery crashes overhead. We run

Ignorant of our ignorance, trampling
Through the burnt tapestry of gorse
 – A patch of sunlight a moment's absolution –
Down to Sker, down headlong to where
The dunes lie between the bay and red
Potato fields, where the house, great
Medieval wedge, stands fused by weather

And memory to the skyline. Here on
The Viking promontory, thin as its
Name and the hail flung off the skerry
We stop, breathless, laughing, looking
Round. We, the inheritors, looking round
To receive what we will never understand.
But beginning our occupation with faith.

from
Life Sentences
1983

Rhys

Best of all I see him in the evening,
The stock of a shotgun cooling behind
A coat, woodpigeon's down plastered
Over his shirtfront: a guilty look,
But laughter under a shock of glossy curls:
Rhys, a squat Mediterranean type
Who kept his dirty tan all winter.

We watched him over the kitchen table,
His son and I, as he broke down
A carburettor, the black grease oozing
From the opened valves, pieces of wrecked
Motorbike spread over the yard.
He talked of the job in the tinplate works
And the way the glowing metal sheets,

Incandescent as lava, came rolling
Towards him, the taste of his own sweat
In his mouth. That was the living
They gave him. Much better the one
He made himself, tuning the huge
Coughing Triumphs to full-throttled song,
Spinning them round in deafening

Rodeos over the mountainside,
Or setting out on evening expeditions,
Bringing us with him in a race downhill,
Glimpsing the moths he dashed from the grass,
Rising like sparks and vanishing,
Running headlong down to the invisible
Ffornwg, its high current moving east

And away, a crown of foam winking
Like beer-froth. And then he'd slip aside,
Deft hands and a murderous purpose
Opening the wire around private land,
And I would wait, thinking of the pigeon
Plucked and headless, the rusted bones
Of metal that he wrenched from the machine.

Driving in Fog

Driving in fog I part the crowded air,
Then the night falls huge and white across the car.

It is as if I stopped believing in the world
The dark conceals, preferring the immense, cold

Flowerings of fog the headlights stain
To dull amber, the solderings of rain

That glisten on the crawling vehicle.
Yet I never seem to break its streaming wall,

Never reach that moment I can rightly say
Here it begins: always it remains a yard away

In the blurred crowding of fields that overhang
The road, the pale entangling yarns

Of my own breath. Here is not the rain's
Assault, the sullen-strange communion

Of the snow. This is no weather but the bland
Present's arrest, for even the trees stand

Like inked letters half-erased. All traffic
Stops. The fog's white sweat gives radiance to the dark.

In a shrunken world I wait for it to pass,
But the fog like countless faces crowds the glass.

Catching My Breath

At midnight I walk over the bailey-bridge,
The mallows waving in dark plantations
Below me at the river's edge, the finest
Paring of the moon quite red above the town.
There's nothing I can say that's praise enough.

No feeling yet, but a new perspective.
I've spent all day in the labour ward
Listening to the women endure a rhythm
Of pain and gas and pain, the sounds from
Their own throats desperate as the cries of the newborn.

For twelve hours then, a spectator
As astonished fathers trooped out of the theatre,
Square rugby players in knife-edge blazers,
A mechanic with a sparse teenage moustache.
And all had stood where I have done

Strapped into gown and mask, watching
The beating of two hearts pencilled on endless
Tickertape, observing a woman's fury and despair
With strange dispassion. She came with a cry,
The sudden child, her skin like grapeskin,

A blue colour, the head fist-sized and punching
At the air, the long birth cable trussing her
Like flex. Now from my place on the bridge
I see the river-shingle gleam under water;
There's no feeling yet; only a place where it will be.
I lean on the parapet to catch my breath.

An Address

1

There is no name, only a faint number,
A position in the middle of a terrace;
But instinct, unerring now, can take me there.

It needs the attention I can't give,
This respectable town house with window
Bays dazzled in evening light, some devious

Cracks in the plasterwork. It shows its age:
Bricks are weathered to a porous tan,
Mortar dry as ashes drifts out of the walls.

2

I'm home now with sunlight barking my skin,
The woodgrain curling white where I plane:
The same process. I could love this work

Of lost causes, a stuttering attempt
To hamper time, repairing a door,
Spreading the acrid varnish over

Parched wood. I look up at walls that need
Repointing, the mesh of crooked tiles.
Even the garden's failing, the beans'

Black flowers a sparse crop in their drills.
I've scared myself on trembling rungs,
Crept through the garret's dark to a snapped fuse,

Blowlamped wainscoting. So another owner
Leaves his mark. Rough carpentry today
Perhaps postpones the fall, but I think

Of tools left hanging on their nails.
At night boards creak. Some pressure on the joists.
All the creatures of this house talk in their sleep.

On the Headland

1   The Thunder Light

November and the hotel hardly breathes.
The drinking rooms are full of winding-sheets.

All morning as the sea echoes retreat
The shoals stand reeking, dark as nicotine,

And a lake of gulls, in flood, in cool recession
Shines across the long shelf of the sand.

Yet anglers stand as they have always done
Like sentries on the breakwater,

The green-walled harbour where the sluices
Shoot the smoking brine into the ebb

And silt rustles like money. It's this
I watch from a beach-head hotel, amongst

The flora of its quiet lounge, and this
That completes me. Winter allows only

The eyes to live, it is a pageant without speech.
And far beyond the sand and low-tide's reach

Is Somerset revealed in a thunderstorm,
The blue light shattering on its cliffs

As faintly now an echo reaches me
Of the air's combustion, a single smothered shot

Dramatic as the coastguard's cannonry
That sometimes breaks the small hours like a child's cry.

And from this place of retiring life,
A brass- and oak-filled room, a group sits puzzling

At the concentrations of the thunder light
In finest shafts that glow like soldering.

Perhaps from there the brightness of this coast
Also surprises, drawing a gaze to this resort

Where young men's exhalations mist the glass
And leaves darken like meat. Out there

It is finishing, the prelude to the storm.
The air tightens with clean desperation.

2   *Cwm y Gaer*

An unknown but suspected world:
Saw-bladed grass, the silken run of sand.

Once the sea's cold level covered all
This hollow place: silence like a great stone

Rolled over the world. And now it is heat
That has the mastery here, a heavy

Velvet muffling limbs, the seamless
Sheath our bodies glisten through.

And everywhere the human print
And everywhere the absence of humanity.

Only this sulphur-smelling rock,
The fossil-beds of erased life,

A leaf of bruised, ecstatic peppermint.
Casting my voice the air rings like a glass.

3 *Sker Point*

On this bleached day even gulls are mute;
The waves rush to the feet like lathered dogs.
And yet I court bad weather, the avoidable
Blast driving me to this needlepoint of rock
Where old red sandstone breaks the wave
And ice blisters the pelting sea-gutters.

Then I kick over a mussel-shell
Luminous with the tide's use. I would be
Like that; allowing in a little light,
Reflecting one thin ray. On the headland
The sea's white coils fall from the stacks,
The wind lances against the raw eyelid:
And in my palm this mussel shell opens
And shuts like a clasp knife, the true tempered blade.

4 *The Sea-Anglers*

The steel lines of the night fishermen
Whip over the harbour rail, the casts
Suspended in waves they cannot see,
A black swell crumbling on the mossed wall.

The hotels have emptied, the bleached
Villas subsided into blankness.
It's an invisible world they fish tonight,
Father and son on their narrow ledge

Where the capstan sits, the tips of their
Enormous rods glinting like spearpoints.
No words connect them, only the steam
From a thermos, the satisfaction

Of their own invisibility. There will be
No fish just yet, merely these two figures
On the promontory encountering
A silence in themselves, disarming

Them of all relationships. In each man
Something invulnerable stirs;
And for the hundredth time tonight
Lines that were stiffened like hawsers

Go slack against the incoming tide,
A calm water where spreads imperceptibly
The white barrage of moonlight
As the shoal moves towards its execution.

5   *Gale Warning*

Irish Sea, Viking, Fastnet, Lundy:
The radio voice is speaking the gale
Warning over mutinous static.
    So buckling into an anorak
I hurry out to our own corner
Of the disturbed Atlantic,
The air full of the pistolcracks of breaking waves.

Only fools would venture here tonight
But I cling to a stanchion and watch
The sea's ramparts grown higher than the town
    Fall back into creamy rubble,
The heavy amber beam from the English
Coast sweep over this turbulence.
Yes, the storm excites, but what is dangerous

Tonight is myself grown ugly,
Unable to think. Today this was
Another country, the olive sand
    With its fleece of bladderwrack,
Spilled oil covering the beach
Like drops of blood. Now I walk to the rail
And look into the quarry of the waves, feel

The town shake under new detonations.
But even the storm is puny. I can laugh
It off, wandering the drenched promenade,
    A body thick and cold as brass,
Wordless, formless, and only this
Knot in my head that I cannot unpluck;
A gale warning, the ache of bad weather.

Burmese Tales

After the swim I move across a beach
Pale as stubble, searing underfoot.
Each wave I remember as a garment
Thrown aside, a chill skin of water
Stiffening into salt and cracked sunburn.

The small sand leeches cling against my legs,
Transparent bodies I watch slowly
Darken like mercury with the blood heat.
And I recall again at the same age
This was my father's daily occupation,

Washing the scum of mangrove-water
From his skin, applying with a surgeon's
Neutral skill, or holding Bogart-like
A cigarette to the feasting creatures,
The hot tobacco shrivelling fat leech-flesh.

His Burmese tales show lurching muleteers
Packing across a spine of hills,
The squads of dark, unmilitary Welsh
Arriving at a village strung
With the waxen rosaries of shrunken heads.

Some things there are to salvage from the waste.
History absorbs this too, and yet
It is his own perspiration I feel chafe
As he lifts the webbing on a green
Insect-thrumming dawn, sucks air. And endures.

And I could go on and on with him
Following the mules through the Shan states
Until the trees become China and the war ends.
His life my drama in the skull's arena.
But such imagery the one inheritance.

from
The Dinosaur Park
1985

The Dinosaur Park

Padlocked, green-white, the villas
Glint like bone in the dusk.
The road a dead end but here's a path
Snaking between houses to a public
Garden. Its lawn's a rug of frost
Behind chainlink where crocuses
Have pushed through stems, white as
Cigarette-papers, the knifepoints
Of their colours; the cold meths-blue
Of steel, a fringe of darker blue.
The path moves on by turnstiles
And a locked kiosk, a bowls sward
And the asphalt tennis courts.
It winds around the dinosaur park.

Off-season and it's shut. I bend a wire
And trespass over frost that shines
Like candlewax. Hummocks and trees,
And then the other trespassers,
Bolted on to sandy plinths,
Moored in the wrong time.
Out of the fantastic past they loom,
Great engines seized, the inert
Mechanics of some botched experiment.
Absurd, abject, the dinosaurs
Are the unimaginable fact.
I pace their world of huge pretence,
The museum quiet grown around the town.
And yet, what's real, as real as these
Vast creatures poised about the park?
The olive plastic of their skin
Under its icy lamination
Is dimpled like golfballs, their
Footprints shallow concrete moulds
Of birdbaths, ashtrays, litter traps,
The eyeballs livid as traffic lights.

History too must have its joke.
They're cartoons come to almost-life,
The dinosaurs, or might belong
To some children's crackling screen.
I've passed the park a score of times
But never glimpsed in its entanglement
These postures struck of combat,
Rage, the slow acknowledging of pain.
And strange to think such creatures shared
The common factors of our lives,
Hurt and hunger, fear of death,
The gradual discovery of betrayal.
But prey and predator are one
And are swallowed up by the omnivorous dark,
The watched, the watcher, and the mammoth's dazzling scythes.

Now level with the dinosaurs
The path runs on, there's no way back,
As shadows make their imperceptible surge.

On the Llyn Fawr Hoard in the National Museum of Wales

for Martin Reed

The fish slide through the lake's cool grip
As the buttresses of Craig y Llyn
Throw shadows on the water,
The orange quilts of spruce dust underfoot.
Piece by piece the hoard is recovered:
Iron black and twisted as fernroots,
Cauldrons spilling their memorials
To ancient sunlight, millennia of seeds,
The pollen of two thousand buried springs
Emerging from the dark throat of Llyn Fawr.

Redeemed from that cold lakewater
They lie in white electric pools;
This spearhead's mottling leaf colour,
Its shaft missing, lake-eaten,
Sickles like the beaks of swans
Worked in inextinguishable
Bronze light, a sword's metal
Burned charcoal-black, the pattern
Of erosion delicate as lace.

Presented here no small sophistication
Of the metalworker's art, that art's
Acknowledgement of something greater than itself —
The cauldron's firm belly of bronze
Yellow as roof-moss, triumphant sphere,
The pin-bolts, brooches, weaponry
Offered to the waters of the lake
In sure sacrifice, their molten substance
Pouring outside the cold cast of time.

Yet saved, they are safe, as remarkable
Only as the tools in my own household.
Behind the glass they are as young as I,
The glass that returns my own scrutiny.
History is not this gear of bronze,
Its patina teal-green;
Rather, it is how it was used,
The association of metal and mind.

Dock

Greek and Irish, the shy Somalian
Make common language the city's nasal whine;
Brothers on the wharf as the cargoes
Come swinging overhead: oranges,
Iron, feldspar, grain, out of the sky
The world's tangible gift, a pittance now
As a shadow shift works the freighters,
Alexandra Dock reproachful with echoes
And this south part of the city an empty hold.

In the chart shop maps like dust sheets hang
From drawing boards, and a last technician
Traces blue fathom lines, as delicate
As webs, the irregular shelving
Of a coast eight thousand miles away.
His pen unlocks the sea. It roars in my head.
The compasses stride a continent
From the white edge of its desert coast
To the equatorial heart; a vessel
Manoeuvres into green Bahia,
Its cabins a dizzying fug of languages.

Walking the dock I find that world
Has vanished like a ship's brief wake.
Across the road the seaman's mission
Is a sour honeycomb of rooms,
The walls of dormitories marbled by the damp.
But where the money came ashore
The banks are moored, ornate as galleons,
All dark Victorian mortar
And the sudden frosts of engraved glass,

Their sooted corbels thrusting like
The jaws of Exchange millionaires.
Straight down to the water's edge
The road runs like a keel.

Eelers

Around the wrecks the congers weave
Their convoluted shapes through decks and cabins,
The sea-invaded rooms of unmarked ships.

Oozing, mottled like orchids,
They are appetite in a sheath of muscle,
Ragged as sleeves pulled inside out.

So ceaseless eels haunt colliers and smacks,
The silt-encrusted cargoes of the sea bottom
Until they take the barb, the reel's arrow.

Then each gill is a flower, a pulse amongst
The wounds, jack-knives and lump-hammers
The eelers' armoury, gaffs and shovels

Rise against the instinct of their rage.
And the mouths of eels twist like the mouths of dogs,
Their bodies are branches, bits of hose

Beneath the oilskin of the conger fishermen.
I've seen these crowd the greasy flags
Of harbours when a motor-launch comes in:

Men high-booted, zipped against the wind,
Their catch preserved in melting ice – mackerels'
Blue tortoiseshell like fishermen's tattoos

A sudden drift of bodies over the dock,
And the congers hung on chains, ferociously torn,
Their mouths agape like beaten, senile men.

The Resort

1   *Surfers*

September evenings they are here after work,
The light banished from the sky behind,
An industrial sunset oiling the sea.
I watch them emerge from the last wave,
Young men and girls grinning like dolphins
In their rubbers, surf riders swept
Suddenly onto this table of dark sand
And thrift, the coastline's low moraine.

And back again to the conflict with water,
Wiping salt-stiffened hair from their eyes,
The flimsy boards pitching like driftwood
On the swell, flattening with the ebb.
Theirs, briefly, is a perilous excitement
When the current lifts them high
And they stand erect on roofs of water,
Balanced on the summit of a wave.

And there they glide, untouchable,
The moment of flight and their bodies'
Instinctive mastery lasting until
They are somersaulted into the foam
And they creep to shore exhausted,
Barefoot, wincing with the discriminate
Steps of thieves, aware perhaps
Of something they might have won, or stolen.

2   *Snaps*

After the rain the small rock pools
Glitter like a switchboard.
The girls wait by the photobooth
Until the card of snaps slides down the chute.
Impossible, they clutch themselves

And stagger, hurt with laughter
In a wild circle. All strangers these,
For whose face matches the idea of self,
That coveted identity, closed like a locket,
The first secret? They've snarled and pouted,
Hid themselves behind the mask of the absurd.
The images come glossy, wet,
Like something born.

3   *At The Knights'*

I walk into the bar and see the faces,
Ugly, staring, full of youth's conceit:
I don't look round because they're all hard cases,
But take my order to a corner seat.

Swastikas carved on motorcycle leathers,
The empty cider cans buckled in half,
But L.O.V.E. across the knuckles in blue letters
Admits the joke, the world's ironic laugh.

4   *'The Kingdom of Evil'*

Afraid of the dark, of being alone,
We come here to investigate
The cause of our unease, the root of a fear
That's a common bond; our inheritance.

Heads torn from bodies, limbs with the pale
Glimmer of fungi; and under glass
A simple and ingenious device
For causing as much possible pain

To a human being. The technology
Is plausible but the terror lies elsewhere.
Here are young men with pushchairs, their giggling
Teenaged wives in wild mascara, tight denim,

And the imperturbable middle-aged
Looking in different directions.
The commentary has a neutral tone,
The history of torture like the history of art,

Periods, schools, the great virtuosi
Of the craft. The henbane Doctor Crippen used
Is a quiver of plastic leaves,
The Yorkshire Ripper wears a tuxedo.

At the exit sunlight slaps the face
And all the smirking children wander off
Into the fair. Behind us, in a darkened room,
The tracery of wax restores
A gleaming tear, the psychopathic grin.

5   *The Arcade*

The crowd tight-lipped, the cries from a machine;
Slots and levers and the engrossing screen

Filled with diagonals, science's straight lines
And the faint reflection of the player's face,

A serious child cocooned in concentration
As an army reassembles at his touch.

Time is banished here. An age might pass
Before he makes his first uncertain move

And turns away to look down the arcade's
Hundred panels of flickering glass

And the figures hunched like snipers at the dials.
His score of leaping zeros glows in green.

6   *On the Sands*

Our bodies blur behind the glass of heat,
Sand's unstable element underfoot.
At every breath the same discovery
Of white sea-rocket waving on the dune
And jellyfish like crystal bowls in which
A dark life rots. Who else can know of this?

Slowly as oil the Cynffig slides towards
The sea – a grey treetrunk preserved in salt,
A furlong of bleached rope. And no one
But us out on the sands, the very tip of Wales.
That shell-sound is the motorway, and from
The steelmill's broken plot an orchid's coral spike.

There is a here and now and nothing else,
The present sucks us in. For the first time
I can look around and find a place so strange
Nothing balances it; there is no context,
Yet death and beauty find a fusion where
The dune halts like a burning glacier.

Our culture has its midden on the sands.
The bottles lie around the beach like empty
Chrysalids, sea holly holds the strewn plastics
In a green pincer. So we embrace our time,
And in ones and twos the people tread the shore
Gazing about them, each with a question.

from THE DINOSAUR PARK (1985)

Picking

We break the webs of morning as we climb,
Plimsolls quickly blackened in the dew.
Higher, stooped and creeping now, laborious
As swimmers sucked into the wave;
Then the mist thins out and as we turn
Forty miles of coast swings like a scythe.

Roofs and bridges, a farmyard's sharp silo,
The gas tanks squat as drums across the plain,
And in the west above the furnaces
A tapestry of smokes disintegrating
Like cirrus. But smoking in our hands
Are green-scaled puffballs meshed in webs,
The goldfish-coloured discs of the chanterelle.

We sip the earth. Beneath this mist
Elusive shoals of fungi in the fields'
Aquarium, their silent rage of growth.
We're richer by the weight of plastic bags
That strain to hold the golfball-dimpled
Mushrooms' packed cartridges of spore,
Their skins on ours as cool as porcelain.

The town's a web of tight estates,
And then the guttural street. We tip a field's
Gleaning into newspaper, crumbs and dirt,
The white pestles heaped in a pyramid,
All foetal shapes and icy embryos.
Out of this bag the sting of light,
The tastes that we must labour to relearn.

from *Breaking Down*

VIII

Everything tastes of something else.
I push the plate away but you,
Craving sweetness, lick the tiny
Chocolate splinters round with your tongue,
Suck up the pool of smoke-coloured cream.
A café by a viaduct, enormous
Breastworks split by long diagonals of shade
Creeping like black moss against the bricks.

Something about your face has changed:
The eyes between their bruises look elsewhere,
And faintly now, but intricate as webs,
The wrinkles start to press into your skin.
Smile, and your cheeks are hollow as spoons,
Glance away and there returns that mark
Of ugly concentration, like purse-strings
Pulling tight within your brow.

We drive down through the valley where
The terracing of shopfronts casts
Parallelograms of light. A long time
Since you looked in these windows, and all
The goods have changed. Digital clocks
Show seconds pass in a shower of green sparks,
The stereo decks are piled up like glass bricks.
Only the river runs traditionally,

Tugging its quilt of iron dust,
While an apprentice in a marble room
Saws at some creature's axles of bone,
The falling meat like hanks of red satin.
The day is full of ceremonies
In which you play no part. Its assault
Comes from colours, faces, words, your own thoughts' treachery:
Our claim on you is part of its strangeness.

X

Latin's the fit language for the stars,
Their bright sterility. You named
The constellations as they swung
Over our heads, fuzzy balls of
Galaxies pulsing in a glass,
The Milky Way's fine spiderweb.

It's only now we understand.
You have been looking away from here
For a long time, gently discarding
Us from your mind. You're breaking out,
Becoming what you always were.
And still at times it feels like a betrayal.

XII

A redbrick mansion in its own estate
Of fields and darker shrubberies
Where statues lean amongst the shadows'
Camouflage. A place to change ideas.
That woman, rouged and striking
As an artificial flower, the toothless
Men who mulch their food – their entry
Is made effortless into this
Closed order, secret society.

XIV

We would go there for fossils, the cliffsides
Rich with those shadows of life, ammonites
Curled tight as catherine wheels, the grey bodies
Of rockpool creatures chalk-marks on a slate.
Our chisels freed them from the steep limestone.

Now a taxi takes you to that quiet place
Through a resort still off-season; a child
Plays in a farm beili, dun farrow and
A green silo the afternoon's landmarks.
Such things might stop the heart, or mean nothing.

The weather clear, but you in overcoat
And boots; there's still a sinew in the wind
And surf is booming at the mouths of caves,
The moraines of coloured plastics on the shore
And all the bleached hillocks of sea-litter.

'A good day for a walk,' he says, 'have fun,'
And spins the red Cortina through the lanes.
And then there is only you and the great
Game of forgetting, an act of concentration
Meant to dissolve a life. Like blowing a sparrow's

Egg perhaps, dark, still, and rough as ice
That perfect thing, a scribble on its shell.
So you move against the slow current
And your calves ache as the next wave slaps
Like some cold green fern over your coat,

And then you are in the undergrowth
As the water opens around you huge
Colourless flowers with a choking scent,
A noose of vines that plucks you from your feet.
Soon the roots of the forest are pressed against your mouth.

Tight as an ammonite you lie curled
In the white stone of the bed. A face of chalk,
And salt-stiff hair that brushes can't untie,
Arranged upon the sheet. Do fossils dream?
Tomorrow when you wake we'll talk and talk.

from
The Looters
1989

The Looters

The helicopter cameras
Bring us the freeze frames.
A black sea outlines each peninsula
As snow finer than marble dust
Blurs the steeples of the spruce.
Bad weather, the wisdom goes,
Brings a community together.
Tonight the screen is a mirror
And the news is us.

At a house in Bedlinog
A drift has left its stain
Like a river in flood
Against the highest eaves.
There will be a plaque placed there soon
As if for some famous son,
While the cataract at Cwm Nash
Is a thirty-foot-long stalactite
Full of eyes and mouths
And the dazzling short circuits
Of a pillar of mercury.
An icicle uncirclable by three men.

Abandoned on the motorway
The container lorries are dislocated
Vertebrae. The freeze has broken
The back of our commerce
While on the farms, the snow-sieged
Estates, people return
To old technologies.

Meat is hung in double rows,
The carcasses identified
By the slashing beams.
Each one looms hugely,
Puzzling as a chrysalis

Under its silver condom of frost.
They sway like garments on a rack
When padlocks break and the freezer-
Doors swing out. It is too cold
Here to trail blood, where bread
Is frozen into breeze-blocks
And ten thousand tubes of lager
Sparkle under their ripping caul.
As flashlights zigzag up the wall
Tights turn red and tropical bronze
In each thin wallet.

The stranded drivers sleep in schools,
Their groups determined to uphold
The constitution of the snow.
Families smile through thermos-steam,
A child with her kitten, blue
As a cinder, sucking a blanket:
The usual cast of winter's news
As the commentary runs its snowplough
Through the annihilating white.

Outside, the cars are scoops
Of cumulus, and toboggans
Polish gutters in the drifts.
We never see the looters.

They move somewhere in the darkness
Through the blizzard, beyond the thin
Bright crescent of the screen,
Those people who have understood the weather
And make tomorrow's news.

'What's the Point of Being Timid when the House is Falling Down?'

i.m. John Tripp

Rumour, like blood, must circulate.
In movement it renews itself.

It was bleak, you said.
Wales was on the dole, and nobody cared;

The poets were in the traps
Waiting for the hare to come back;

In the country of the apathetic
The half-hearted man is king.

The fescue bleached, and the spiked bobbins of the teasel
Tip back and forth to the wind's pulse.

You had just made out
A staggering travel-expenses claim;

Train and bus I know give no free rides,
But John, I was driving you home.

For some reason I am digging,
Bruising my heel on the spade's blue shoulder.

And, creature of the great indoors,
It was strange that I should see you last

Walking up the Merthyr Road,
That ravaged sheepskin an affront to Whitchurch decency.

Six inches down I unearth a seam of frost,
Pale as anteggs, running into the dark.

Four in the morning is no time
To rediscover a savage malt;

The barman in pyjamas stared in weary disbelief;
Then turned, found the optics, and pressed.

It's all around me I suppose,
The invisible life of late winter

Accelerating now, an unstoppable rumour.
About you, famous drinkers,

Earnest lyric souls, and the merely loud
Had turned to wax.

There's something here that's at its end,
And something already edging into its place.

Make it a double, you grinned,
Savouring reunion with the Gaelic smoke.

The magpies in the hawthorn repair their dome,
In the barrels ice shrinks to a small dark embryo.

After all, a Sunday in Llandrindod
Offers no mercy to the squeamish.

The Mansion

The house stands as it always has,
Its windows tall above the lake
And grass cut almost to the yellow root.

Along the drive a whitelimed kerb
Follows a perfect crescent,
As if stone, like air or water, moved in waves.

My steps dissolve in gardens where
The acid rhododendron thrives,
Its flowers pink and white as naked dolls.

It always was a selfish tree,
Devouring the light, growing
Glossy and alone, the strong inheritor.

At the door they take my card
And a name in silver italics
Grants entry where I never thought to pass.

These hands laid gently on my arm
Disturb an earlier trespasser,
That child under the yew hedge

Who watched the long cars slide through his village
And women shaped like candleflames
Moving over the lawns.

Above his head the berries swelled
As soft as wax around each nucleus,
The black nugget of poison that would grow.

Epilogue

We bring you apples in a plastic bag
And build a pyramid of offerings
Around the radio. I feel its current,
Bloodlike, faint as breath.

It was hard to find the ward;
I remembered a railway siding
Where the coaches are stalled amongst
Scorching ragwort, and there is
One carriage with its windows broken
And a name sprayed down the side,
As if language is the last defiant act.

But you're not speaking
And we listen to ourselves fill drawers
With the words you don't require,
And all I can think of is you at dewfall,
The hem of your dress in a black hoop,
Plucking the sour champions from the trees
Where lichen is splashed orange
As yolk and hangs its tapers
Of goathair from the bark.

It's only the living that hold me here.
Your gaze goes further than that stubbled youth
With earrings like the silver
Wheels of a watch, holding flowers
And a ribboned box
That will never be untied;
And beyond these spruce-green orderlies

Smoothing out a bin-liner
As if a crease in a child's dress.
They are all too near, or new, for your concern.

But with them I form a circle
You cannot break. You're the stranger here
I will not recognise, a face
Empty as the misted water in this jug.
You've turned away from everything
That I could do or say,
So that there's nothing left to think about
But the yellow beads of applesap
I want to see about your mouth
Before we pack up, turn the channel off.

from *Fairground Music*

1   *Dawn*

The mist comes out of Somerset
And the air turns to ash.
In the rain a man caresses
The beach with the slow
Arcs of a metal detector.
Every morning the pennies
And ruptured cans
Are moments of discovery
Exciting the dial.
But between the squill and the thrift
The single clue today
Is this fine blue plastic
Like the skin of some creature
Grown immense and moved away,
Leaving these fragments of identity.
Only its absence is making sense.

3   *Nuns Bathing*

From the garden to the dunes
Laughter threads their single file.

Brown as fieldfares
They move towards the waves

And climb the sea-eaten wall
For the green pencils of samphire,

Smiling at something not of this place
And sniffing their lemony fingers.

Each one holds a camera.
Their children are already conceived.

6   *Ghost Train*

A paperback novel
Placed cover up,
The headphones pulled down tight
Inside her hair.

No need to talk.
She pushes out tickets with the change
And we step into a carriage
On the rail.

Through the cracks in their fingers
Our children
Squint at oblivion.
The soundtrack's running down like a lit fuse.

And from her hutch of glass
This girl stares out,
The disc of tickets turning on its spike.
Her purple nails
Are filed like arrowheads.

9   *Madam Zeena*

A breeze moves the plastic
Skirts of the hut
As she traces the palm's hieroglyphic.

Under the curtain
The feet of a fast-food queue,
The dabs of paint and effervescent rusts
On the Wheel of Fate.

And at her table
A fat schoolboy, nodding
And pink-freckled as an orchid,
Cheekbones rouged by sunlight
In the chalk of his face;

A lunchtime schoolboy
Awkward and shivering in the gloom,
As the mystery of what happens
Is confessed to him.

12   *From the Summit*

As we fall and rise
On the Wheel of Fate
Our voices are peeled away.

Swinging us above the town
It holds us now an instant,
Breath frozen, upside down,
Staring outward at the roofs
Of cars and aisles of caravans,

Towards that profile of the dunes,
Their neolithic sunset
Through the blue buckthorn.

And distantly, as far as sight allows,
A figure on the beach
Is sweeping a crescent on the sand,
Someone alone, heartbreakingly small,
Who would make the great discovery.

Then machinery crashes
And the whole town's like a film reeled back
As we rush towards the ground.

Men

In the cool Jersey air
The Buicks are nose to tail
On the highway and their horns
Calling to each other like owls.

And the men sit and
Wait, elbows on the rolled-
Down glass, the clockfaces
In the dash starting to glow.
The dusk turns petrol-blue.

They look at the backs
Of each other's heads
As the Boeings go over
With burning lights
And the silver Amtrack carriages
Knife past without a breath.

They stare at each other's
Bristling scalps, the pugnacious
Shaping of a skull,
Seeking out a statement there,
Measuring the distances.
And ahead a horizon
Of refineries, the neon
Signature of *Miller Lite*.

In the Watchtower

The frontier hums, a live
Cable carrying our charge.
Barbed wire and the sentry posts
Bristle against a wall of acid firs:
Climbing the steps I'm brushing off
Their needles hooked into my clothes,
The needle wax's scent of oranges.

It's safe here in the clocktower –
The villagers' dovecote –
Where sunlight varnishes the boards
And soldiers lean their guns

Against a wall, put down
Binoculars and take to twisting round,
Like farmers with a barren hen,
The necks of tall bottles.

And I smile as they step, dainty as girls,
Out of the rifles' harnesses,
Thinking of my grandfather
And the scornful way he'd leave his spade
After a morning's couch-cutting,
Relief flexing through the racked
Sinews, yellower than iris roots,
And spreading from the halfmoons of his sweat.

I've never seen a gun so close,
This grey snub-barrelled thing
Shining like a beetle's carapace,
No bigger than a toy's image.
But touching it might set the bells

Above us, now a cluster of blue grapes,
Speaking the first syllables
Of the last war, and loose the doves –
Preening on the shoulders of bellmetal –
In a volley over Czechoslovakia.

Those fields swim in a blue-green haze
Like the pages of a passport.
I stop, and feel the current stir
Beneath me, two armies praying
To the eager god of electricity,
While a family of leverets
Wild as pinball in the grass
Cross frontiers within sight but out of range.

Looking for Arthur

Now here was a valley stranger than most
In the legends. A heap of rusted cars
Lay racked like toast, and the pool of green
Nitrogen simmered between rocks.

We expected distant shouts,
Some land-manager's pursuit of our trespassing,
But only the silence accosted us
As we moved under the wall of the engine-house,

Higher, it seemed, than a cathedral,
Its gorgeous brickwork prickly with red moss,
And left the known world behind.
The mountain wore a scarf of mist

And below us now the buzzard
Floated like a fallen handkerchief.
I climbed in silence, middle-aged respect,
But the children creased the solemn tarns

With handfuls of the scree, dragging
Wellies through those cauldrons in the peat.
They swung on ropes of voices to the crown,
To discover that we were explorers

Of what someone else already knew,
But to retrieve from the cave's maw
This one horseshoe, whose rusting leaves
As yew-wood does, a regal dust

Against the skin, and glimpse the ocean's
Pale eyelid winking in its notch,
While at our feet a hare lay pressed
As flat as ruined corn.

from
Hey Fatman
1994

Homework

The paper comes off in wet
Streamers, and soon we are down
To the hard plaster, green
And pitted as avocado rind.

Outside, they are building
A temple, their nest a papier-mâché
Face that peers down at us
Through the laburnum's dome of flowers.

We thought it was the perfume
That brought such fever,
The bush a shivering lantern
Of wings, and a scarf of petals

In the gutter below. We sat
Beneath it with magazines,
Tired of the tearing work
Of household archaeology,

Revealing provinces of floral print
And a gothic continent.
And as we ripped, so they returned,
Each time with a wasp-jaw of shining mortar,

Labourers on the wing, the wasp-traffic
Building a swarm-house.
Now how much like a heart it hangs,
Chambered, fiercely beating

With the season's old compulsion.
I'll let it swing there in the fork
Drying like a garlic-bulb
Till winter strips it skin from ruined skin.

Daisy at the Court

'Arithmetic and manners, start with those':
And he had left her on the stair
And gone off after partridges, small bundles
Of feathers you'd tread on before they'd move.

So this was it. A house as long as a street,
Stone lions, and the Welsh language
In a shield on the portico. One of the children
Already pawed the darkness under her skirt.

In a newspaper once she had wondered
At the Cherokee leader who claimed
The worst part of exile was having nowhere
To bury your dead. 'Yes', she murmured,

Picturing homesickness as a white
Lily, one of those flowers grown
For the graveside, a field of lilies
Whose perfume was a secret shared only by herself.

'This isn't home', breathed the nanny, a girl
Whom no child had sucked, thinking of
The charcoal ovens in Dean, no bigger
Than beehives, the warmer vowels:

This was foreign, even the bread was strange,
And at dinner the men came out
Of the greenhouses and looked at you when
Your back was turned. Especially the ones with wives.

And yet. There was Ivor, most often Ive,
(Christian names in this country split in half)
Who saluted every morning, except once,
When his hands were cupped for her in a nest

Of blond apricots; who had walked her down
To a corner of the long garden,
Where water was spun across terraces,
Looped and stretched over rocks, before falling

Like a roll of silk into a pool.
'This is a palace,' he had said. 'At Catterick
We slept fifty to the barrack-room
And still the windows froze on the inside:

'In the village we cut the avenue
Of elms, a hundred years old, for firewood;
There's some eat only gooseberries and milk.
But here is a place hard times don't touch.'

She had looked at him then and felt
All the ghostly answers of a sum unwritten,
As the Wolseley bit into the drive's gravel
And a man leaped out and strode towards her.

A History of Dunraven

1   The Inheritors

With the headlights off,
The tape turned up to max,

The Astra roars in first
Between the warning signs.

From the air the fort's a faint sketching,
Green ammonite in the rock.

There's not a wall, not a ditch
You might point at and say,

Here they persevered, the first ones
In a desperate place, a cliff edge

Mauve with sea-kale, neighboured by
Ghosts and psychopaths, making their stand

On an arrowhead of the cliff,
This limestone buttress, sea-foam

A starry lichen staining its rock.
Was their music solace or the last

Defiant act? That anthem for a better time
Dated them, placing their tryst

In its unarguable context
As they sat, belted in, burned

White, fused to the machine,
Pure as fossils and all the humdrum

Plastics of the shore, and the sea
An uninterested echo, miles out.

2   *The Ice Tower*

They packed it in straw,
Carried it on paddles to the kitchen,
Were grateful for its constancy.

And in its cellar
Ice comforted itself,
Fed like grief upon its own image.

Ice was master
And mistress in this tower,
Its ridged wall the colour

Of dragonflies, its sweat
Pearling the darkness,
The gutter running as it sloughed

A snakeskin of glacial
Purples, ebb-tide greys.
I listened, said the scullery-maid,

Hurrying down from the castle
One June evening, the gorse
Ecstatic as goldfinches;

And heard the sound it made, a lover's
Groan, something I should not say.
I rushed out to the gatehouse

Frightened of a footfall
Not my own. But there was nothing.
Only the tower behind, its door bolted

And my poor hands raw
From where I had sawn the blocks;
No splinters, yet the slow needlework of blood.

3   *Temple Bay*

No statuary or white marble
But all the same a shrine,
Sabrina's villa in a crook
Of the bay, the gramophone's
Hissing jitterbug, a champagne
Bottle in a glove of frost.

And sometimes, the king himself,
Hilarious, well-wined,
Plunging to the shoulder
In some inscrutable pool,
Or shiggly on a limestone sill
Cruel as razor-wire.

Behind him, the black
Hexagon of the cavemouth
Where the kitchen-girl, nipples budding
Through a beach-dress frilled
Like a sea-anemone, calls him back,
Their picnic danced flat in the sand.

4   *Red Data Book*

Lists mainly, in shaming Latin.
Epitaphs for next year. Next week.

Of course, there are peoples too
Who might be honoured in its pages:

The Kreen-Akore, the Mandans:
Their stone-age pinioned by cameras.

But of the inhabitants of Dunraven
Only one is named, *falco peregrinus*,

Gwalch glas, peregrine, the slayer
Of racing fowl, fox of the loft.

I saw Enoch Powell once, tiny,
Squat as a goshawk, shaking

With rage as he described a plot
That had done him down.

The crowd was not prepared to blink. It knew
The danger there like a rank smell of its own.

And every June the peregrines
Quarter the cliff; ultimate ferocity

With nowhere to go. Their beaks
Are tin-openers for the sternum,

Clawgrip an iron-maiden lock.
That sort of purity can't last.

Meanwhile, in the Non-Political,
For the second night, three men spread maps

On a table-top, open a jewellery-box
With a satin base, soft as a bean-pod:

Think of the agate that could nestle there;
The garnets. They dint the fine material,

Prepare a place of honour
For two warm, white stones.

5   *A Kind of Jericho*

Down in the fruit-garden the children
Were smelling the currant bushes.
'Poultices,' said Annie. 'Tomcats,' smirked the boys,
'Or outside privy after Miss Pritchard
Has come out, smoothing her apron.'
'I'm glad I'm not a bee,' shrieked Annie, tearing off,
Back to the packing cases, the impossibility of it all.

Every day for a month the square green van
With the gold lettering had edged down
The cliff road, past the gate-house, and then up
The castle ascent. The driver carried
A bottle of tea; his young men had basin-cuts
And talked about the *palaver*, the *malarkey*.
No complaints though. This was serious work.

They dropped a mirror, nothing fancy, in the courtyard.
Its abacus of icicles lay
Uncleared all week. That said it all.
Milord was upping sticks, putting lot-numbers
On the centuries. In the laundry-rooms,
As big as any estate farmhouse, they were
Coppering the winding-sheets of Dunraven.

Impossible to say now who got what.
The sets of blue Nantgarw were knocked down
To a hundred collectors. There are thatched
Vale pubs where the silver heads of ibex
Frame the video screens. And when the blizzard
Ceased, everything from the catalogue,
Down to the last cracked po, had disappeared.

Yet this was only treachery's prelude.
What remained was the castle, quoined
On a promontory above an ocean
Chalked by porpoises, hostage to leisure.
A team of quarrymen were hired, who placed
Their dynamite under weight-bearing walls,
Consulted for days on the angles of collapse.

A mile away the crowds could feel the tremor
In their knees, saw a flower of spray
Conceal the house. And when it lifted
There was a hole in the world.
There were some who picked for years over
The moraines of plaster the explosions built.
And some who have cursed a plague-plot.

Hey Fatman

Me? I was only watching. Nothing else.
It had been one hundred degrees that day
And I'm not used to frying. So I took a seat
Outside and ordered a drink.
The beer came in a glass like a test-tube,
The colour of that monkey, the golden one,
They're trying to save around there,
The one with the mane like a lion.
And Christ, it tasted cold as a dentist's drill.

But after a while I felt the energy
To look around. And I saw
What I expected to see from a street like that:
The last soccer players on the beach,
A big surf pounding, angry, futile
In the place where it always stopped its charge,
And a beggar eating fire,
Walking up and down outside the restaurants,
A magician folding banknotes for his pimp.

At the bar stood the boss in a mildewed tux,
The sweat hanging off him in icicles.
He looked at me once and passed over –
Not important, not a player tonight.
I ordered another to make him doubt,
But he never blinked. You can't buy style.
So I studied his empire's neon sign
Out on the pavement. There was a moth on it
With wings like two South Americas.

It was bigger than my hand. But either
Nobody had seen it or nobody cared.
I wanted to scare it off that scorching globe,
Grab its wings like the old man's black lapels,
But it was impossible to move.
I couldn't get out of my chair,
Couldn't speak. So I sat and looked,
With a radioactive thirst, at the bar
And its imperceptible protocols.

The women were in by now, four of them
At the counter, each holding a drink
With an hibiscus flower in it, and a straw:
One white, one black, two mulatto,
Like my beer. In ones and twos they'd get up
And stroll outside to the pavement,
Amongst the tables, sometimes out of sight,
Wandering around the expense accounts,
As the city's electricity came on.

They weren't collecting for charity,
That's for certain. I couldn't understand
A word, but I knew what their smiles said
As they squeezed past, what their fingernails
Meant as they chimed against glass,
The stick-on ones, red as foxgloves:
Hey fatman, that's what they said;
Almost without saying it, if you know what I mean.
Because that's all it takes in a place like that.

Their earrings said it, their crossed
And uncrossed legs: and off they'd go
With the turks in singlets,
The executives in their button-downs,
Up a darkened stair behind the bar,
And the old man there in opera black
Would smile with his blue iguana lips
As he held the door for them, then pulled it fast,
His armpits dimpled like a garlic-press.

Ten minutes later you'd think there were four
Different girls. Not so. The younger ones
Were older now, the brunettes reborn as blondes.
And they'd suck their drinks and circulate,
Trailing a perfume through the room
Of their own sweat, like a herb crushed underfoot.
Hey fatman, it said to the night,
To the brass propellers of the fan
That uttered ceaselessly its quiet scream.

I watched the moth float down like charred paper.
Over the walls the baby roaches ran
Warning of fire, waving their brown arms.
Down through the haloes in my glass
I saw a furnace glow, the table blistering.
A man in the mirror tried to douse his boiling eyes,
But the women of the city combed their hair,
Buckled on silver, strapped on gold,
Then stepped once more out on to its hot coals.

Reunion Street

I jump from the step of the moving bus,
Trying that schoolboy trick again.
And touch suspicious ground.
This is a town where the past still waits
Like a mocking class behind the teacher's back.
Too many people here can claim my time;
I might glance into a shop window
And see the reflections go on forever.

Goosebumped, I know there are ghosts about.
And, after thirty years, Gareth, here you are,
Bald and expansive in a cape,
A *cape*, for God's sake, uncertain now
In the crowd between the taxi office
And the dark corridor of the video arcade
Cheeping like a battery-farm, the half-term kids
Silent at the coffin-shaped machines.

Bald? I feel my own crown thin, find
Sometimes, unbelievably, a silver
Spider's web on a shirt worn for an hour.
But bald as bath-pumice you stand there,
Perhaps a few pale strawberry hairs
All that's left of the auburn fringe I remember,
Your pudding-basin trim, a bristly tonsure
Scary as a fontanelle, apparent even then.

I like the cape, its tent of tweed
Clasped by a thick bronze pin.
Ridiculous, maybe, but I'll admit
The style, the courage it takes to fight
The wrong way up a street of nudging youths
With barbed-wire scalps and toxic-bright baggies.
You stretch their hair's breadth tolerance:
I like that too. They think you dangerous.

This might be home and yet it's hard to feel
At ease. The library's computerised,
And the old books in a trolley under
Polythene. Can't give them away, Gar,
A whole decade of second division literature
Hardly date-stamped in a job-lot in the rain.
Books die like people, odorous and slow.
I see their pages curling, silver in the flames.

The last time I met you was over chess.
We used a Victorian penny like black glass
As one of the pawns, pushed a dimpled
Thimble for a rook. The talk of boarding-school
Struck me as a simple, clean betrayal.
The other boys were right. Here was a snob
Who'd been to elocution class, whose family's
Politics were bluer than their swimming-pool.

But who cares now? This six-foot-something
Heavyweight has the same wise-owlish air
As the boy who urged me kneel to meet
The chilled, subterranean eye
Of a viper coiled beneath zinc sheet,
Stoop to a reef of fungus in the wood,
Each tree girdled by an orange
Scentless aureole our penknives sliced like bread.

They've shut the flicks, that shrieking coop
Where Jason and the Argonauts fought off
The skeletons. The music in the town's
Long gone, and beer is a desperate nourishment.
Perhaps that's why I stand concealed
And watch you swan up Market Street –
Baffled exotic on an ebbing tide –
Scared by the questions you might ask of me.

Listening to History

It is there again –
Scissors on the grindstone,
Death rattle of an electric bulb.

Somehow it sounds familiar
But I cannot quite remember
When I last heard
The cog so busy on the spindle.

The dusk puts old age
Into my eyes. From this dune
The fields are dirty banknotes,
A biker on the sands
An angry maybug drawing a helix,
And the thousand white faces of the burnet rose
Impassive now, almost bored,
Like a crowd at half-time.

Yet I know it is down there,
Crouched along a pine branch
As flat as a piece of tortoiseshell
And still as the green, fletched cones:

Goat-sucker, night-crow,
Milk-stealer, fern-owl,
Neolithic footprint
Next to the hiking-boot,
Coif of bracken, coral eye,
And the lost voice searching
For the one who might know it in all this din.

The Swimming Lesson

'Out of your depth,' the instructor warns,
But a man might drown in a thimble
Is my philosophy. And for a second
I am sublime. Weightless in a cradle.

'Deep breaths,' she shouts, and now I taste
Blood and oysters as the sea swallows
Me, its invincible salt rubbed in
As I thrash in the shallows.

'Breathe,' she says, 'you need to breathe';
But my body is drawn
Taut as a broom-pod before it detonates.
So this is what it feels like to be born,

I think, before the luxury of breath,
To stammer on the brink of real speech.
And face down in the sand I count
The lipsticked Marlboros that paint the beach

Like sea-rocket, the international
Brand-names discarded by the tide.
This is how I learn to save my life,
To doggy-paddle, porpoise-glide

Into the nameless spaces on the map –
Eryngo-blue isthmus, canal
Of starving eels. But lesson over
I still hold to something more predictable.

'Ah, it's not my element,' was what
I always said, a poor excuse
From one who read no horoscopes,
But not unwise. I knew what might douse

The sun. And so for thirty years
I side-stepped with a genius
All attempts to make me swim.
School was worst. At the local baths,

Brutalised by chlorine and the guards'
Insolent musculature
I would sit in tropic changing rooms
Clutching a forged letter,

Whilst next-door the baffling shouts of joy
Drowned the mutter of the pipes.
Even the nunks and fatties swam,
The twitching academic types

Excused from outdoor sports, a ridiculous
Stick-insect in borrowed costume
Braved the deep-end's fathom and a half.
I watched the clock, immersed in shame.

Water, of course was not to blame.
I happily trawled the tannin-
Coloured streams for dragonflies'
Barbarous larvae, the sharp sewin

And minnows thin as pine-needles,
Always an inch beyond a fingertip.
Waist-deep in that cold current
I'd not trouble how a simple slip

Could dunk this non-swimmer
– Hydrophobic with a bucket of young trout –
Under the Ffornwg's dark plumage of weed,
And keep him there until the light went out.

Somehow, this was different:
A homage paid to a primitive god.
Swimming itself seemed as ludicrous
As flying; quite alien to the blood.

So for thirty years of foolishness
I kept myself to the dry ground.
I never sought that stream again,
The civil war of water and the land.

Now England's the set for a commercial break.
Ten miles out of London, signs warn
Of deer crossing, and here the forest
Is primeval, soft with lichen

Strung like bladderwrack. Where the trees end
Is the Jolly Fiddler carpark
And Rod Stewart's Lamborghini,
A scarlet flick-knife in the settling dark.

Under the saloon's low eaves
The drinkers watch the pipistrelles
Ricochet off walls of air, hear Essex
Chime with evensong's electric bells.

A traveller here, I still look twice
At machine-guns worn on airport stairs
And a man guarding rare orchids
With chainleashed rottweilers.

But that's England now, and we have stopped
Amidst its eastern breweries
For pizzas from the microwave
And surly pints with yeast thick in the lees.

The mansion here is short-lease flats,
Plasterboard and flaking gloss
Dividing like a honeycomb
The hall and drawing rooms. A Polish

Caretaker waved at the gatehouse
As traffic brought home office-
Staff and counter-clerks from Harlow,
Parking beneath a high cornice

Of gargoyles, next to leaded panes.
Bedsitterland in Borsetshire
Was how my friend described the pile,
But I was only eager to explore.

Carp nudged the lake's candelabrum
Of lilies, the vines lay thick
In nettledust. Yet the pool was perfect,
Brimful in a courtyard of glazed brick

With diving-board and spotless changing-room.
Dragged daily by the caretaker
Its oval shone in starlight
Like a polished ballroom floor.

That's how I see it still, a pool
Immaculate under lunar
Continents. I crouched to stroke that silver –
Like the hymen of a coffee-jar –

And felt no old unease.
Adnam's had seen to that of course,
And several shouts of Breakspear's
Chased by unwanted Scotch.

Salacious midnight drew us on
Towards the unlit mansion house,
Yet the last idea of the day
Seemed one of genius.

Clothes and shoes lay where they fell,
And naked, done with merriment,
I submitted to the shallows' manacles.
Water handles us like a parent,

With a hard, incomprehensible love.
Stiff in its embrace we gasp
For air, choke on impossible
Explanations. Think to escape

And the way we came is covered
By the same rough tide that holds us;
Hate it, and it pulls tighter, our
Nostrils burning with its phosphorus.

There was nothing in the water now
But blackness. I saw my hand on the surface
As if smoothing out the pages
Of some brand-new atlas,

Hesitant strokes to brush away the dark.
The others were invisible,
The sparks of their swimming extinguished
Somewhere at the frontiers of the pool.

A swan, a lily, both are moored
By fury and tenacity
To life. But seeking their mirage of grace
I found instead an icy

Millimetre of pondwater
Beneath my heel. And clearly in that slow
Capsize, I saw the sisters venture
To the beach, laughing, years ago,

To the sea's nunnery, all raw-boned girls
In sheaths of black and glistening plum,
Embracing the first weak wave.
I walked the bay where they had swum –

A knucklebone behind the town –
And heard again their gentle ribaldry,
Saw hair piled high in alice-bands,
Their sealheads all miraculously dry.

Then a fist of water took me in the throat
And an electric bulb shone all
Its hundred watts against my eyes,
The filament a red tongue inside a skull.

Hearing the silence, I think I cried;
If so, the words sank useless as iron
Into the pool's still sanctuary.
And there I was a boy again

Bent above a shadow on the stream,
Ragged fringe over the face,
Buttocks pale and thin as willow-leaves:
A hunter in a nameless place.

So thirty years of foolishness
Ended as I dragged my body in,
Spitting the pool's astringency
And moonlight like a nettle on the skin.

from
After the Hurricane
2002

The Bombing of Baghdad as seen from an Electrical Goods Shop

Eating was serious work.
I watched you arrange as an evening ritual
The hummus rough with lemon rind
And bread dusted with Jordanian thyme.

Every supper, you said, might be the last.
So maybe that's the way to live,
The way that we should read our books
Or view as now at home this notch of sea,
Silvered and thunderstruck,
Between the pillars of the esp,
A ladle of spelter hissing at the air.

Nazaar, I know the market place today
Must be quiet as the British Cemetery,
That field with headstones of forgotten boys
Who died of cholera and Baghdad heat.

There's no haggling with the smoke-seller
Or the women with switchsticks, flicking
Flies away from Tigris bream:
The honey and grapes and Syrian soap
Are stalled in convoys along the border road.

And I suppose that you're at home,
Because where else is there to be on a night like this,
Listening to the Cruise missiles, the only
Traffic out tonight on Palestine Street,
While here in the window of Edwards Electrical
Your city in the tracers' glow
Becomes a negative of itself.

Twenty-Five Laments for Iraq

The muezzin voices break the night
Telling us of what we are composed:
Coffee grits; a transparency of sugar;
The ghost of the cardamom in the cup's mosque.

★

These soldiers will not marry.
They are betrothed already
To the daughters of uranium.

★

Scheherazade sits
In heat and dust
Watching her bucket fill.
This is the first story.

★

Before hunger
　　　Thirst.
Before prayer
　　　Thirst.
Before money
　　　Thirst.
Before Thirst
　　　Water.

★

Boys of Watts and Jones County
Build cookfires on the ramparts of Ur.
But the desert birds are silent
And the wolves of the province
Fled to the north.

★

While we are filming the sick child
The sick child behind us
Dies. And as we turn our camera
The family group smartens itself
As if grieving might offend.

★

Red and gold
The baldaquins
Beneath the Baghdad moon,
Beneath the Pepsi globe.

★

Since the first Caliph
There has been the suq –
These lemons, this fish:
And hunched over the stone
The women in their black –
Four dusty aubergines.

★

My daughter, he says,
Stroking the Sony DV cam,
Its batteries hot, the tally light red.
My daughter.

But his daughter, 12, keeps to her cot,
Woo, woo, wooing like the hoopoe
Over the British Cemetery.

★

What are children here
But olive stones under our shoes?
Reach instead for the date
Before its brilliance tarnishes.

★

Back and forth
Back and forth
The Euphrates kingfisher,
The ferryman's rope.

★

The ice-seller waits
Beneath his thatch of palm,
His money running in the gutter's tilth.

★

Over the searchlights
And machine-gun nests on Rashid Street
The bats explode like tracer fire.

★

Yellow as dates these lizards
Bask on the basilica.
Our cameraman removes his shoes,
Squats down to pray.

★

Radiant,
With the throat of a shark,
The angel who came to the hundreds
Sheltered in Amiriya.

★

In the hotel carpark
One hundred and fifty brides and grooms
Await the photographer.
All night I lie awake
Listening to their cries.

★

This first dollar peeled off the wad
Buys a stack of dinars higher than my heart.

★

A heron in white
And a woman in black
Knee-deep together
In the green Tigris.

★

Her two pomegranates lie beside the bed
But they have carried the child away.

★

She alights from the bus
In a cloud of black,
The moon and stars upon her skirt,
And painted across her breast
The Eye that Sees All Things.

★

The vermilion on his toenails
Is almost worn away,
This child of the bazaar,
Who rolls my banknote to a tube
And scans through its telescope
The ruins of Babylon.

★

Four billion years
Until the uranium
That was spilled at Ur
Unmakes itself.
Easier to wait for the sun to die.

★

In the Ministry of Information
Computers are down, the offices dark;
But with me in the corridor
A secret police of cockroaches.

★

Moths, I say.
No. Look again, she suggests.
Fused to the ceiling are the black hands
Of the children of Amiriya.

★

Sometimes
The certainties return:
These cushions, a pipe,
And the sweet Basran tea
Stewed with limes.

The Discovery of Radioactivity

When Monsieur Becquerel returns to Paris
He takes out a key and unlocks a drawer
In his desk. Then he understands.

It is as if the black stone he had placed there
Is breathing. Something has come out of it.
The hot soul of the stone squats in the dark of the desk.

One hundred years later
I edge the Astro as far as the barbed wire:
The road ends with a warning sign

With the warning worn away.
In the prickly pear our geiger starts to percolate.
It is as if somewhere the junco, somewhere the chickadee

Were scolding us. But Daniel speaks
Our instructions. Stay here too long
And we'll give the daughters of uranium

A bedroom in our bones.
So no one lives here now.
No one will ever live here

But the desert poltergeists –
Thorium, Americium, each a wild child
Run off into the world,

Performing great deeds, performing terrible deeds,
But beyond us now, strayed forever out of reach.
Ah, Monsieur Becquerel, help us to understand.

When our sun is as small as the heart of the prickly pear
The atoms of your black stone
Will still scintillate,

Compulsive as that key you finger
In the pocket of your waistcoat,
Impatient on the journey home.

Carioca

It's a 127
      Going to the Rodoviaria
And the driver tapping his head.
He's saying I'm loco, I think:
      Loco,
      The locoman,
And as usual there's a crush

So already her breasts
Are pushing into me –
      A gold ring
Between the cups of her bikinitop –
Her face a thin carioca's face
      But the body
      An oiled cuirass;

And the bus is bucking
Among the taxis on Avenida Atlantica
And outside the children of the traffic islands and tunnelmouths
Are sharing bags of manioc and beans,
Sucking fishbones thrown from the lanchonetes
      And the driver is pulling
At his eyelid,

      Look, look man
And at last I understand,
      But her hands are so swift
I cannot feel
The razor slitting the bagstraps
      Or the velcro
      Opening its cat's mouth,

But my hands are against her breasts now,
      Beautiful travesties
            Silver as phosphorus
      And her eyes a centimetre away

Irreducible shots of the barraca's
          Aguardiente –
     Those first sips

     That lighten the head
And stiffen the knee –
And her smell a mansmell because I know that smell
Then somehow she is through the turnstile
          And I am shivering
Like a hummingbird shivers
          Over its own image.

Songs for the Lugmen

1

     Weeks
Of high pressure.
Even the earth is foreign.
But in these caves I discover
The sigh of the subterranean ...

Then, on the Weather Channel
A swell off the Azores.
     And we feel it.
          We feel it.
The Gulf Stream in us roars.

2

Two lovers lie beneath the stack:
Wiggling like wheatears,
          their arses white
Against the rock wall's black.

And the lugmen laugh
And come down the sandy trail,
The tyres of their bicycle
Hissing, the young one looking back.

3

In the dunes, nothing grows taller
               than a man's arms aloft.
Our desert is a golden tarp
                       thrown over limestone.
More memory there than Microsoft.

Around us this pampas
Of viper and thorn,
          the cinnabar moon
Grinning like a computer virus.

4

The lugmen have taken off their shirts.
How pale they are;
              and faded their tattoos.
The older cycles through the surf,
Handlebars hung with shoes.

And I come later, wandering
The long line of their pits,
Each with its hillock
             of nickel-coloured sand
Where the sea circulates.

5

Ah, I have tried to comprehend
          the orchids' telepathy.
But their thoughts are lightning bolts
          earthed too deep for me.

Yet in these caves I overhear
       the gods of limestone whisper
Before the sea begins its climb
       like a shining escalator.

6

The younger lies upon his side
With his arm thrust in the sand.
Now there is a serpent, blind
And silver, wrapped around his hand.

The old man waits, holding the pail.
Lug are lug; he knows their ways:
Even the big villains, dug from their crypt,
Can no longer amaze.

7

How far down is out of reach?
              Li-lo,
         marlinspike,
Drowned abbot's crozier
Are sunk together at the roots of the beach.

So the lugmen smoke and dig again,
Oblivious of the bathers,
The mothers and children sat in the surf,
The solitary fathers.

8

The future lies beneath their feet,
Laid out in this savannah
Where the coming and the going meet
And transform one another.

from AFTER THE HURRICANE (2002)   99

The lugmen on their knees
Are listening at the pools.
In their bucket I see vitriols;
Lenses that look through geologies.

9

There they crouch into the breeze, mouths pursed like anemones.
Salt and samphire on the tongue
But how briefly lasts the lozenge
Of language.

They seek no scenery.
Only the pools of Ffynnon Wen
Where the thief and the murderer
Are baptised again
                and again.

10

Above us is the thunderhead
And suddenly a sky
Pulling itself inside out.
The crowds have turned away.

So who knows what the lugmen know
Or if what they know contains
The beginning of weather,
                the ending of weather
In Africa's red rains.

She Drove a 'Seventies Plymouth

She drove a 'seventies Plymouth,
Great barge of a thing –
Chrome erosion, filler in the wing,
Rust like a sour tooth.

It was thirty below
And on Second all the stopped traffic
Was throttling out goosefeather exhaust
Thicker than the snow.

But I had to stop dead
On the sidewalk, new workboots
Rubbing a heel. And what do you know
If I'm not staring straight into that automobile

At this native woman, hair
A black fan under her tuke
And every fingernail painted red.
Or something I prefer. Magenta.

I eased the fit and watched her
Take out a white pencil of salve
And moisten her top lip with the care
Of a little girl colouring in.

Then the same with the bottom
Lip. Then all around in a bright
O. I could taste it myself,
That ointment. Sweet jism.

She saw me in the mirror.
I was one yard away with the tongue
Out of my boot. So what are eyes for,
I'm asking? There's nothing I done wrong.

Neolithic

For an hour I watch the sea
        tear itself apart
then go back by the ridge,
gold dust on it, carrion on it,
a tower of fallen sentinels.

      And honest to God
   I swear, though already in a moment
memory will reinvent itself like duneland fire
      suddenly
            she is there
grain by grain forming before my eyes,

Her skin and hair, the pinched face
        and the tattoos as small as insect bites
        and a little feathered purse that might carry her Samsung
        and the child with her
dark skinned, waving a gull's wing
and the sand a spinning tube, a helix –
little twister that writhes into a child.

   Then last of all the man, a head taller –
a stick and a pouch with yarrow in it for their wounds
  – a magician we would call him –
on the dune where the sand blows around in little ecstasies,
but the grains move again

And their bodies
        dislocate
      and blur
      and the family falls apart
into the stone that smells of sulphur
and into the corals they go, into the orchid
mouths, into the grass with blades
       pale as wishbones
into the umbilicus of sand the lugworm leaves –

three genies back into the bottle
of the bronze age, three faces disappearing
        shocked
    as the burnet-rose,
        blackeyed.

Don't go, blackeyes, not a handful of sand remaining;
        not a grain.
            Don't go.
Must my gentle breath destroy you?
But in the ghost train the siren is sounding
and the skeletons are shiggling on their wires
and now there is no one left but the jet ski boy
carving the symbol for infinity
        white across the bay.

The Porthcawl Preludes

Salt

Pray to the inexhaustible.
Sip the venomous vintages.
The first
        and true
        Religion of this world
        Is thirst.

The Drowning Man

    Over my head
    The grey pages
    Float down from the photocopier.
    How could I ever have doubted
    The sea's apocrypha?

Neap

Surfer, cursing the calm,
Oystercatcher beeping like a smoke-alarm,
    Anglers weighting their lines:
Now and forever the sea's concubines.

Oyster

Tonight there's no mistake:
Moonlight on the wave
            is a sunken Taj Mahal.
Within me now the ache,
The premonition of the pearl.

Foghorn

I am the call to prayer.
So let us now consider
The sulphurous god of Nausea,
The ivory god of Enervation:
Today's ruling deities of the ocean.

Buoy

Forever voicing melancholy
Let my fate prevent your folly.

Ammonite

Like you I dream of a tropical coast.
        Unlike you I see
        The prefecture of fern,
The spunkhot churnings of Gondwanaland.

Lighthouse

I fly a kite around my head,
A restless, broken thing.
Is no one there who'd let me rest,
And take the silver string?

Razor Shell

Allen Curnow told me this
And it's the best advice you'll ever get:
    Never turn your back
    On an ocean.

Creel

I prayed for a mermaid,
And, God's truth, in she climbed.
I'd hold her yet in my oubliette,
A voodoo child of Port au Prince,
Black as a cormorant, her eyes
Shining like comb jellies.
But...I awoke, beached...uncrated
And even the dream is dehydrated.

Rock Pool

Where but this mirror would you find
Forgotten youth, imaginary joys,
The selves your single selfhood left behind,
Those indigo girls and boys?

Meteorologist

I watched the sky turn opera black
Over Misteriosa Bank. And the ocean?
That first wave would have filled a cathedral.
  Because what is science after all
  But prayer with our eyes open.

Dogfish

I am sprockled
    Like a foxglove,
        My teeth
A silversmith's hammers.
Yet, like you, I will be overwhelmed
By the rip tide in the blood.

High Water Mark

The office junior spilt my tea,
Is good at office mimicry.
When I confessed I'd die for her
She told the girls on the tenth floor.

In corridors I see their eyes
Sated with their own surmise.
When the e-mail comes from Personnel
I'll tell them all to go to hell.

Iceberg

Here I drift, golden as a mosque
Through the noon heat of Baghdad.
  Dark birds descend upon me
  And on every thoroughfare
Pilgrims stagger backward from my shrine.

Jellyfish

I once saw
Your white disc lift from the prairie.
Now here you are again, the moon's
Placenta, washed up on the shore.
   But what is this within you,
Your heart, your brain, or your nuclear core
Small as a saskatoon?

Cardiff Bay

Lobsters in the market tank
Crawl slowly round the sand,
But look, their claws are tied together
With elastic bands.

Scorpion Fish

O my Chinese grandmother,
Would it be so hard to smile?
All the lagoon is your sugar cake.

Driftwood

The wine has gone out of me.
The grain has gone out of me.
The sap with its mosquito cry
Has gone out of me.
And all my petals pressed
Within the book of tides.

Surfer

Fjords? *Cwteri?*
Every isthmus
    A temporary
        Parenthesis?
So much contained by so little.
    Like our own skin.
Marine biology is an apology.
    The sea's within.

Sand

  Ah, girl in a red scarf,
Writing your name into geology.
  Before I forget you
The continents will come to rest
  Like broken butterflies.

The Drowned Man

I drank the sea.
It drove me mad.
But now I know
It was the serum for my dreams.

Nautiloid

  Life's a beach
  For the *nouveau riche.*
  This sea's not what it was.

Basking Shark

There is an ocean on the moon, I'm told.
A blue ocean of dust, aeons old.
Perhaps there are sharks there, basking in the swell.
Yeah. Moonsharks in moondust. Who can tell?

Salmon

Look closer.
That is not the new moon
In the net of Orion.
I leapt too far.

Pearl Fisherman

I stand on Euclid Avenue
Before a thundering train
And dream of the sands of Nicobar
I will never see again.

Coelacanth

You and I –
The ugly sisters.
And who is this between?
Time, of course, the kitchen girl,
Radiant in her rags.

Dolphin

The salt has dried on me.
Soon under my skin the roses will erupt.
  But still I smile, teeth
A bloodied knuckleduster.
Now, like all the rest of you, the sea
  Creeps up to look.

Shell

Once again, the girl in the red scarf.
What shall I whisper
When she raises the northern hemisphere
To her ear?

Coal Miner

Two miles out I lay
Like a holothurian, in a beam
Of its own phosphorescence.
  Or a fossil that would squeeze itself
  Back into the seam.

Starfish

So, golden one.
Do I bow or can we shake hands?

Turnstone

    Windscissors! Triangulator!
For the first time mathematics
    Stays in my head.
Think what Pythagoras would have made of you.

Shag

Dark little abbot on your rock,
You will have to preach louder than that.
These days the congregation is a long way out.

Doldrum

The office junior has long legs
Like the girls in catalogues.
Such compliments should have their place
But now I dread her sour face.
    Does mercy move her fingertips
    For an effigy in paperclips?

Blue Whale

I know my fate:
It is loneliness.
I feel it moving
Deep as the Gulf Stream around me.
It makes me great.

Sea Anemones

Meanwhile, at a standpipe
In the fourteenth district of Baghdad
    Three sisters shake the water
    Out of their electric hair.

Message in a Bottle

After a generation on the swell
    You uncork my tiny scrap:
Instead of X upon the map
    Stands your name, indelible.

Bathysphere

With my ruby eye
I looked into the abyss
And learned that language only lives in light.
So who will make the words for what I saw?

Buccaneer

I sailed on a schooner to Tristan da Cunha,
   Broke an embargo around Santiago,
Pirated spices off the coast of Maroc.
But now I'm more of your stoic than superheroic,
   And prefer The Pier to a Norwegian ria,
Or doing the conger around Tusker Rock.

Wreck

The sea took my handbag
And emptied it over the shore.
What's left now but a tissue, a ticket
On the Jurassic's ballroom floor?

Prawn Crackers & Oyster Sauce

It's dark.
Take off your clothes.
Move into the first wave.
   Just *sohh*.
Now move into the second wave.
Admire your newfound phosphorescence.
   And listen this last time
To the sea's
      Chinese
            whispers.

Horizon

It shrugs its golden epaulettes;
Daylight's petition is denied.
Are we the ones the shining world forgets
Or are there watchers on that other side?

From the Rock Pool

1

One night an arm stretched into my room.
It was the lighthouse beam
scattering a handful of salt.

The next night the hand brought
a child's bones
burning like driftwood with a small white flame.

The third night it set down
my own biography:
thirteen white pages in a white book:

On the first page of that book I wrote:
what could a rock pool ever be
but a bridge that serves the selves?

2

Last week at the airport I met the sea in Terminal 1.
She was drinking Finnish coffee and reading the Dead Sea Scrolls.
On one ankle was a tattoo of Australia
while Greenland was inked in blue over her breast.
This is fate, I said. Do you come here often?
And I stared into the icebergs in her eyes.

Fate, she said, has nothing to do with it.
And if the Welsh could swim
    they'd be Irish.

3

   I held the microphone
to the water. And now I can play the sea's voices
at night. At night an old tide
rides next to my ear, its
grand co-ordinates, its inexhaustible
mutterment. But the sea's language
is what the heart translates:
a tango under the cliffs,
Twentieth Century Fox's heraldic chords.
   Here in the rock pool
   I have conducted them all.

4

In the Apollo I was dancing with a woman I had never met before.
But when I brought our drinks back from the bar
the sea was kissing her arm, the sea was touching her hand,
the sea was sliding her fingers over her hair, her long black hair
that smelled of almonds. So what could I do? Tell me, what could
I do?

What could any man have done?

The concert was terrifying.
All I heard
Was high tide crashing
In the orchestra pit.

Then yesterday
There was a seagull's voice
On the answer-phone.
I think it was a kittiwake.

Kneel a moment
        and watch below –
look, there in the undergrowth –
those lacerated lives.
Their eyes and their hands know the deluge
is due.
        But I –
        I know nothing.
I stand in exile
watching my footprints disappear
like breath off the sands.
        Nothing that leads up to me
        has lasted.
There is no baptism here:
there can be no consecration.

There is only what the tide leaves:
        a Sanskrit of coal,
        a McDonald's plastic lid,
        an empty hourglass.
Until the next of times
        and only the next of times
these too have their appointed place.
        But I who was born in the rock pool
know nothing has lasted.

7

Today the sea is dressed
as my doctor's receptionist.
You must have an appointment, she says.
Without an appointment there is no one to see.
 If you have no appointment
 If you have no appointment
 If you have no appointment
  you do not exist.

8

Should I wait for wisdom here?
I could write on a napkin
all that the sea has to say.
The sea that knows every atom of herself.

 I made a tape
 of the book of tides.
 I could play it to the concert hall,
 to the computer,
 to the sky,
 yet only the heart
 might translate.

9

Midnight, I was shopping in Tesco
down the aisle with the starfruit and the figs,
down the aisle with the chimichanga and the burritos,
down the aisle with the black bread and the white bread.
And I could have sworn…
I could have sworn
but every time I looked around
there was only an old man, a young woman,
a child with a windmill.

I could have sworn…
I could have sworn
but there was only an old woman, a young man,
a windmill turning round.

10

Somehow the sea discovered my mobile number.
When she rang me at work I had to go outside like a smoker
and then pretend it was a call from the surgery.

11

I stayed in my room one hundred years
until I heard a knock on the door.
There stood the sea in torn denim
asking me to come to the cinema.
We watched *The Beach* together
but it doesn't mean we're going out.

12

Who are you? I asked the sea.
Sister of the desert, she said.
The same salt,
the same.

Who are you? I asked again.
Lover of the moon, she said.
The same salt,
the same.

What have you seen? I asked the sea.
An iron sun
inside this world.
An iron sun.

I have seen diamonds
smoke on an anvil,
civilisations slip
through pavement cracks.

Dry as ice I lay
between Europe and America.
Below me the stone breathing,
the stone's breath.

13

Now I know
there is an apocalypse
    within the rock pool.

Now I know
there is an apocalypse
    within the rose.

14

My doctor held the stethoscope to my heart.
    And heard the surf.
The doctor wrapped my arm in a black armband.
    And felt the tide.
The doctor squeezed my balls with a plastic glove.
    And talked to me of drowning.

Now, every day, the e-mails, the text messages
from C. But who is C?
C is a stalker, C holds a grudge,
C has mistaken me for someone else.
We must meet, writes C.
But who is C?
Soon, says C. I'm coming so very soon.

15

One day I dreamed
   I will turn on the light
and the sea will have flooded the kitchen;
   I will switch on the computer
and the sea will have filled the screen;
   I will go to my bed
and find the waves waiting in their heartbreaking underwear.

16

Sorry, but I have stopped counting the faces
   that swim into this pool.
They wait as if I was an oracle
   but what can I tell them
that they have not already heard
in the whip-weed,
or driftwood's liturgy?
   Listen, everything that will ever be said
   must stand on a pillar of silence.

17

   Today, like a *torero*
the sea wears a suit of mirrors,
arsenic and gold in her pockets
and the names of the drowned
in a sequence of sequins
   she has sewn into her sleeves.

18

Yet there is a rhapsody
   within the rock pool.
Look here, vines with their air-grapes,
a harvest of breath in the fresh air vines
and the vineleaves wrapping the surface,
   the pool's sky.

   And the sunset?
Think of the tip of Isaiah's tongue
while far to the south-west
the Gower peninsula
   is a ballet shoe
   with the satin worn away.

   You understand?
I have learned to open my eyes underwater,
I have learned to look where there is no light,
gazing down through the waves in my green goggles
as if I peered at a solar eclipse –
as if the sun had cooled blacker
   than all the blacknesses of the seabed.

19

In the Funland arcade I stood next to the sea.
I lost every coin in my pocket
but the sea kept winning money all afternoon.

Lend me a dollar, a dinar, a shekel, a groat, I asked.
An escudo, a euro, a forint, a florin.
A pound, a peso, a crown, a cruzeiro,

Lend me a Skanderbeg beggar's qindarka,
that I can play this game until the end.
But the sea said nothing. Instead she knelt down
and the money-child ran laughing into her arms.

20

Today the sea is dressed as a bride
    who wears black:
a black train of ashes follows her down the aisle,
    she holds black flowers
that were picked at midnight on midwinter's night.
    When she kisses me at the altar
her tongue goes deep inside my throat
blackening every word I've ever said.

21

Trust no one on the shore.
Not the gull with its eye
    like a papaya seed,
not the fishermen who come to judge,
quiet as the crowd at the crucifixion.

Instead, we must dare the tide.
We must dare the tide.
No matter if it takes eternity
    we must count the roses
    within the rock pool
    and the rock pools
    within the rose.

22

    On millennium eve
we stroll on the sand at Kiribati.
How we love these islands, the sea and I,
    and how we love the language
of the islands and the thirteen letters
of its alphabet.
    Ah, the lucky thirteen.

Yes, if words are coral,
then languages are islands,
I tell the sea. You have yours
    and I have mine.
But the sea only smiles
and holds my hand tighter
    as we walk together into the sunset.

from
The Adulterer's Tongue
2003

Belly Button Song

*For Fflur, after buying that most worthless – or valuable – of birthday presents –
a belly button jewel*

Of all the buttons I ever opened, you were the one
that like no other, undressed me.

That little wound tucked under its plaster
hid a bloodspot as if left by a safety pin.

For a while it seemed a tribute to a clean cut
before we separated and grew inseparable.

The belly button? What is it but memory's whirlpool,
a summer cloud between us, the little white clock

of ecstasy? But when you were born
you discovered a world that's full of buttons,

some silver, some brass, some that hold us tight or strip us bare.
What's sure is, late or soon, we're all undone.

But such a mystery you were, a little sensor
that can tell me the world's temperature,

and now I see in this blue nail in your navel
a tiny screen where I might watch you whole.

And if flesh allows us what the flesh allows
how might we ever know loneliness,
counting buttons, like the stars, between us.

from 'Botwm i'r Botwm Bol', by Menna Elfyn

Taliesin

A sparrowhawk, soaring, I saw
Argoed's English auguries
and so predicted an army of days,
suns' pale faces above shields' black rims,
an empire built of empty eyes and mouths,
and I felt a wind cold as the corpse-skin
of our brotherhood.

Then I was an eagle, going somewhere else,
when I flew over Flanders and remembered then
how the future would look,
the next day's gridlock in the trenches,
the wound-psalms, the filth-prayers,
the mothers like nervous serving girls
at the grave's banquet.

Not long ago
I was an albatross, patient above Port Stanley,
seeing Galtieri's boys
discover what the end of time feels like.
And now comes another crowd,
their boots melting on the Baghdad road,
and the whole world watching
through a dodo's eye.

from 'Taliesin', by Emyr Lewis

Beginning to Forget

This is the moment the *sigl-di-gwt*
turns into the *wagtail*.
I watch her carefully
while the stream screams scandal
over the mountain
but there is no one in the village
who cares for such news

And of course the wagtail pays
no attention to this.
How self-assured she is,
as usual reserving her reverence
for light, for earth only.
This is the bird I've seen
vanish quicker than
a dropped consonant.

Meanwhile it's *swallows* from now on
above my head.
Once there was nothing sexier
than the squibbing
gwenoliaid of Cardiganshire,
their corkscrewing wings opening the wine
of twilight. Their language
was written in my spirit:
their chorus the sound of being alive,
deeper in me than any words of mine,
or any silence, any pain.

from 'Dechrau'r Anghofio', by Gwyneth Lewis

Landscape without a Hat

Purple moorstream all down the mountain,
and the moss like a redhead's sideburns there.
But here's me gasping, gutted, grape-
skinned, catching my breath in a plover's scrape.

In purple moorstream I went to wallow
without an inkling there was incense there
or of the nubile in the noble
in that high Sargasso of mountain grass,

where now I shimmy like some ocean
creature, reeled up and joyful, even
to the eaves of the sun, as down
in the dewpits the dawn ignites the grass.

Thus in your purple hair I stand
unable even to cast my shadow
over these falling waves, speckled with seeds,
of purple moorstream that breaks across

all my aching consciousness,
sinking every certainty
upon a moorland rock; for what are you
but the silver thatch of a wave,

you, whose warfare is the tide,
my God of spindrift blessings.

from 'Tirlun heb Het', by Bobi Jones

A Song about Soup

Look, I'm not singing about soup,
and certainly not that saviour's
savour, or any bonemarrow stars on the soup's surface
and their enticements to the tongue.

Listen, because I'm still not singing soup,
or broth's puckering beatitudes
or all the archaeology of taste
or the steam's psalter swinging over the stove.

Because, after all, soup's only soup,
potatoes, meat and a jug of stock,
there's no exotica from the Larousse index
or sundried Mediterranean glossaries.

No, I'm definitely not singing soup.
But instead maybe something half recalled,
as if with an instinct for the indistinct.
So I sing the spoon, I sing the bowl –
the summoning tools of a ritual
that might release
soup's secret soul.

You see? This was never a song about soup,
its superlative suns and their salt eclipse.
And absolutely nothing to do with a warm kitchen
where a place has been set for me.

from 'Cawl', by Elin ap Hywel

Automobiles

It's a scorching May morning in Memphis
and there's a pileup on the interstate
with a body splayed out not even twitching in the sun,
and all this parade on hold
with a Chevrolet pickup, windshield
stove-in, waiting in some kind of vigil.

It's early but Graceland's gates
already receive the first sinners,
the King's zealotry scrolling down
their registers of grief at his monument,
while beyond the graffiti
and traffic's metronome
a pink Cadillac stands unhotwireable
out on Elvis Presley Boulevard
awaiting the resurrection.

By sunset the Lorraine Hotel's a fiery
doppelgänger of itself in Peabody's department glass,
and under the balcony where Martin was shot
the carneys and the conmen are shutting their stalls,
and some woman, trying to keep his flame alive,
collecting for the homeless,
while the Olds and Pontiacs
that brought the prophet here
a quarter century ago
are submarines in shadows
at the end of the hot afternoon.

American heartbeat, American breath;
the dark cortèges idling in the dust.

from 'Ceir', by Iwan Llwyd

from
King Driftwood
2008

An Opera in Baghdad

1

Here's a feather.
Made of fire.
Where's my father?
Made of fire.
All this fiddle.
Made of fire.
Fat and fifty.
Made of fire.
Fuddy duddy.
Made of fire.
Flesh alfresco.
Made of fire.

2

Saddam?
He ran
dressed as a beggar.
Dressed as a businessman.
Yes, Saddam Hussein, he ran away.

The Imperial Guard?
They ran too.
Those hundreds of the brave,
those hundreds of the true.
Yes, the Imperial Guard, they all ran away.

But the water boys there, every one of them stayed,
every one of them pissing themselves, every one afraid.
And they smoked and they swore and they gambled and they
                                                        prayed.
The water boys there? Every one of them stayed.

They kept a canary down there in the gloom,
and it sang day and night in that terrible room,
as they tended the pumps that sent out the water
and they tried to forget the abominable slaughter.
Yes while the bird sang, like a shower of rain,
they forgot about Bush and Saddam Hussein.

You can call them the traitors, you can call them the mad,
but those were the best men there were in Baghdad.
They gave us the water when that's all we had.
Yes, they gave us the water, in the midst of defeat,
when the smart bombs were flying down Palestine Street.
Yes, they gave us the water when that's all we had.

3

Just bones.
High and dry.

So I sulk.
Just bones.

But the black stars
inside me now.

The black stars
all inside.

Too soon. To the sun.
Too soon.

So blood boils. On a bed of nails.
Flesh fails.

The silver tongue.
The iron lung.

And I die
high and dry.

4

The Tigris and the Thames. The Tigris and the Thames.
That's what I see, the Tigris and the Thames.
The Tigris green as kingfishers.
The Thames all sparrow brown.

5

I stood one night at Rotherhithe
and watched the river writhe,
the river writhe in Rotherhithe
and heard the barges creak and the drowned girls speak
in the Thames at Rotherhithe.

But as I made my way down Palestine Street
I smelled the wide Tigris,
the river smell that lifts the air
in a city such as this.
Then down on my head fell the barbarian sun
that knows no armistice.

6

Deep in the bunker at Amiriya
I learned another word for fear.
That's where I went to hear the truth.
That's where I found the baby's tooth.

    A milk tooth,
blue as a cinder. And it whispers:
coward, whose pain is it anyway?
Your cells are a blizzard,
your mind a rag book, yet
I dream you into growth
luscious as papaya flesh
around my black seed.

Why this need to condemn what you find here?
You will carry me now
as a part of yourself.
In time I will feel your bones
gasp in their foundry,
and at night, you do not know,
but I will hear your blood
like a bench of silversmiths
pause at its work.
Then continue.

Forever now
I will ache in the skull
of the man who stooped in the shelter
of Amiriya to pick the tooth
of a child like a rice grain
from the ash.

7

The Tigris and the Thames. The Tigris and the Thames.
The Tigris black with blood.
The Thames all black with blood.

The Tigris filled with oil.
The Thames all filled with oil.
The Tigris and the Thames. The Tigris and the Thames.

The Tigris green as kingfishers.
The Thames all sparrow brown.
The Tigris and the Thames. The Tigris and the Thames.

8

As I made my way...
As I made my way down...

As I made my way down Palestine Street
I watched a funeral pass –
all the women waving lilac stems
around a coffin made of glass
and the face of the man who lay within
who had breathed a poison gas.

As I made my way down Palestine Street
I heard the call to prayer
and I stopped at the door of the golden mosque
to watch the faithful there
but there was blood on the walls and the muezzin's eyes
were wild with his despair.

As I made my way down Palestine Street
I met two blind beggars
And into their hands I pressed my hands
with a hundred black dinars;
and their salutes were those of the Imperial Guard
in the Mother of all Wars.

9

Here's a free man.
Made of fire.
Every feature.
Made of fire.
Forty footsteps.
Made of fire.
Full of feelings.
Made of fire.
Every fibre.
Made of fire.

Now a flower.
Made of fire.
All his fury.
Made of fire.
For a phantom.
Made of fire.
All this fear.
Made of fire.
Flesh alfresco.
Made of fire.

10

The Tigris runs through marshes where the herons are white.
The Thames runs through the marshes where the herons are grey.
The Tigris and the Thames. The Tigris and the Thames.

But I never drink the water. No, I never drink the water.
Of the Tigris. Of the Thames.
Of the Tigris. Of the Thames.

11

As I made my way...
As I made my way down
As I made my way down Palestine Street
I smelled the wide Tigris,
the river smell that lifts the air
in a city such as this;
but down on my head fell the barbarian sun
that knows no armistice.

As I made my way down Palestine Street
I saw a Cruise missile,
a slow and silver caravan
on its slow and silver mile,
and a beggar child turned up his face
and blessed it with a smile.

As I made my way down Palestine Street
under the yellow palms
I saw their branches hung with yellow dates
all sweeter than salaams,
and when that same child reached up to touch,
the fruit fell in his arms.

12

Find a fountain.
Made of fire.
Fill a funnel.
Made of fire.
Fluorocarbon.
Made of fire.
Ferro-concrete
Made of fire.
Fuck the future.
Made of fire.
Find the fossils.
Made of fire.
All that's funny.
Made of fire.
Full of feasting.
Made of fire.
Here's a feather.
Made of fire.
Where's my father?
Made of fire.
All this fiddle.
Made of fire.
Fat and fifty.
Made of fire.
Fuddy duddy.
Made of fire.
In this furnace
of the fire.

13

But Radiohead said.
Radiohead said.
Creep, they said. Creep.
A creep crawls.

But I fly. I spy.
An arrow
To the atmosphere.

The bends. My friends.
I'm sent. Blood-bent.
Blood rends. The bends.

Creep, they said.
A creep crawls. Dragging his chains.
But I fly. Too soon.
To the sun. With these pains.

A stone. A megaphone.
Blood bent I'm sent.

High and dry and high and dry.
I die.

With the black stars.
The black stars.

14

The bird in its cage sang an ancient maqam
of flowering fountains and rivers that ran,
of the rivers of Babylon, gentle to man.
Yes the bird in its cage sang an ancient maqam,
for those men in the pit who already seemed damned.
For the men who were doomed but continue to stand.

Yes they gave us the water when that's all we had
as it all went to hell on the streets of Baghdad.
They stayed at their posts in the fiery city,
maybe for love, or maybe for pity,
yes they stayed at their posts in all of that slaughter
because they were the men who worked with the water.

You can call them the traitors, you can call them the mad,
but those are the best men there were in Baghdad.
They gave us the water when that's all we had.
Yes, they gave us the water, in the midst of defeat,
when the smart bombs were flying down Palestine Street.
Yes, they gave us the water when that's all we had.

They kept a canary down there in the gloom,
and it sang day and night in that terrible room,
while they tended the pumps that sent out the water
and they tried to forget the abominable slaughter.
Yes while the bird sang, like a shower of rain
they forgot about Bush and Saddam Hussein.

The Hourglass

Biding my time.
        Biding my time...

Third lesson in the high school and I look up suddenly.
I have taught in this room for thirty years
and told children about coastal erosion
and how there is order in the universe.

But I am growing old in their service
while my classes remain young.
Forty, fifty, but the girls
always seventeen. And the boys twelve.

Hottest Day Ever
says the *Manchester Evening News*.
    I close my eyes and think:
tomorrow is Thursday. I will not come in…
    I will never come in again.

Now, what's that?

    That sound?
      It's sand
in its auditorium
    applauding itself.

Because sand can do anything.
Yes sand can do anything
but sleep.

The land slips by.
    Lordy, how the land slips by.
Cliffs on castors and rocks unriveted from immemorial plinths,
    scenery teetering
as on some vaudeville stage.

    Sand,
you were Nebuchadnezzar once,
The Lords of Dahomey. Now, sleeping off the latest sesh
    which you will not recall

a street cleaner rousts you with his broom
in the gutter behind The Buccaneer.

    Yes, there lies sand,
    a haemophiliac boy
    with highlights in his hair.

    Sand,
you were the special one.
You took the Sphinx to fifteen rounds,
out-manoeuvred Ozymandias from the first.

More grains in you than words in Wikipedia.
　　Ah, virgin under the veil,
you are the necromancer
writing backwards in an upside-down book,
a magpie that drops a golden quoit into the latrine.
　　That's you, sand.

　　So has sand
sinned? That shifty gait, such wry
restlessness. A guilty conscience,
　　I suspect.

When the beach travelled past at twenty-five miles per hour,
knee-high, white and whispering, going east,
I thought it a sail on some argosy.
　　Yet how strange to think
I live in a country that is leaving me behind.

And yet, such energy,
you know what I mean?
I need, I want
sand's amphetamine.

　　Suddenly the sky
purple as toothwort.
　　Deadbolts drawn
but sand already in the freezer,
the safe behind the portrait of the Laughing Cavalier.
　　Ah, it's your nature sand:
fox and scorpion learned their ethics from you,
your glacier approaches like the Rawalpindi Express,
　　a simoom grinding its gears.

　　Yes, I thought, sand
　　is a library: sand is
Prozac Nation, *Ecclesiastes*, *The Dream Diary of Teenage Tanya*.
　　But sand is also *Das Kapital*
　　with the punctuation taken away.

That heavy breathing on the phone?
It's sand, of course, bored with being alone.

I had dialled the sand chat line.
What a mistake. Now the calls come
every night. Every day the texts, the threats.
        Sand sold my number
to the sea. I'm thinking of coming round,
says a voice. Because I know
        where you live.

        How sand gloats.
        Since carbon copped for us
        we sulk for silicon.

    At Kenfig the fog
        fell in a golden
Götterdämmerung. The swan, the sanderlings,
the conger cold as cistern-iron?
The famished sand filched that feast.
And the poets who practised there left nameless;
well-drivers, grapegrowers, wolfwatchers likewise.
    If any escaped
they are unrecorded. Only the castle sometimes
    is mistaken in the mist.
How drunk was that watchman
he missed the dune at the door?

A simple question. Or so I thought.
Who is the saint of sand? I asked.
But sand only stared at me, thin and unsunned.
You need a holiday, said sand at last. I know just the place.

How far, I asked of sand.
    How far? As far as
the Sahara's final finial.
    That's how far.

On Olympus we passed
the poets weeping
into their websites.
We wanted fame, they cried.
But not for this. Not this.

Every winter at Punta Ala
when the villas are shut up and the restaurants closed
sand would stride up the beach and into the *pineta*.
This time I was sand's companion
and we moved farther than ever before
and came upon a field of sunflowers:
a thousand sunflowers black in the moonlight,
ten thousand sunflowers in their ruin,
each face a black zodiac,
an army of sunflowers leaning on their spears,
some spell upon them,
an enchanter's curse or a draught from a poisoned well.

A child was singing in that midnight
and we stopped to listen to her Etruscan lullaby.
Behind us stood the lighthouses of Napoleon's island,
on and off. On, off:
tall as sunflowers, I thought.
And then sand laughed.
Because what is buried must be revealed
and nothing stays a secret long.
Or so said sand of that dark syndicate.

Moab might be Lot's grandson and massive ordnance air blast
but tonight it's the mother of all burgers. Yet soon that neon
charcuterie is left behind as we climb to Chapel Road and in the
Datsun start to crawl round the haçienda.

Headlamps off, we're a black car in unpolluted darkness. The
house too is unlit. The gates are closed and there's no guard.

But then, who is that? Up there in the tower? A figure is
gazing, skywards of course, ever skyward, the telescope barrel
pointing north east. So I look with it.

Hey, where did these come from? Such raw constellations:

the Cactus, the Cadillac, the Habanero. I've never seen them before.

Got to be Cage himself, hisses sand. Built the house specially, didn't he? For the sky. The empty sky.

So while Nicolas Cage is scoping the sky we're stalking the stars. Yes, Nick Cage. I think of him in *Leaving Las Vegas*, tipping that quart into himself like it was mother's milk. As if he was filled with ashes and he opened his mouth to a cloud-burst. Call it irrigation. As if he was filled with sand.

Okay, maybe in reality he's not so great. Those sad tattoos? But you have to have a model, see. A role model. And Nicolas Cage might be mine. Because Cage built an observatory. And now he's up there looking at all this; the fireflies, the UFOs, the shakedown of meteors over the desert.

I can picture that glass he brandishes. Black lens with a rain-water meniscus set in a gold bezel. So I'm here too, sneaking with sand round his villa in the piñon pine and prickly pear, an audience outside his theatre. Because where else should we be, tell me that, when rising from the rimrock is this midnight moss of mescal-coloured stars?

But so far, said sand,
everything has been displacement activity.
There are great things to which I aspire.
One day they will be revealed to me.

Here is a clue.
    How the arboreal
        bores me. If a leaf's first life
is grace then fast falls fire and grief.
    The olive and the baobab
are bones under my battering ram.
Ahead I smell a country of oaks
and orchards, that rumour of silence
        amidst skeletons of the spruce.

Remember, I was in Eden too,
said sand. The snake squeezed over me

and I felt it as I feel children's fingers writing their names.
That serpent slept lidless in a cave while I kept guard
    and whispered to it.
              If only
you knew, I told it,
                  my every grain is red
                  as a pomegranate.

Okay.
    I confess.

I thought sand a lost cause.
            No visa,
        no English,
     no hope.
But there it was on the slipway,
the sudden sand in sodden silks.
How could we send it back?
(Some tried poking it with a stick).

        Here are the signs
        of catastrophe:
     magpies at their pillage;
     burdock dark in the barley;
soon, a pittering, a pattering upon that green leather
polished for a century by every parliamentary arse.
Next, the Prime Minister rubbing something from his eye.
    It is with regret, he says. So much regret...

You might drown in a drop
I heard sand explain,
not thinking I
could be crushed by a grain.

And always towards:
that's how sand moves, always
towards and never away.
Never back, even in retreat.
Even in retreat
it's always towards.

Yes, I thought. It came in a flash.
What sand teaches
is that there's no oblivion.

So consider sand,
that sorcerer full of secrets.
What shape should sand assume?
A girl in beads, braids and barrettes?
Sumo, sapsucker, the old Sumerian writing the law?
But I saw sand acting up in Arcadia's aisles,
Lou Reed's 'Perfect Day' on someone's mobile
and all the jackpot silver still untouched.

The second time I went officially with sand
we passed through the checkpoint at Lukeville.
Two miles into the desert I watched a soldier pull
a Mexican boy off the back axle under a bus.
An illegal, see. One of the legions of *La Lucha*.
And all following the north star
above *El Camino del Diablo*,
past the Barry Goldwater Airforce Base.

I looked into the eyes of that soldier and he was twenty, max.
Biding his time. Biding his time.
But in those eyes I saw the prehistoric ash
and glimmering fulgurite of every desert place.
He was a sand man, see. Oh he was one of us.

Of the twenty-six ahead, counted sand,
fourteen are already dead, seven of thirst, seven from sunstroke.
Their tongues are black as the pumice stone.
One man, seeking shade, has pushed his head
into the badlands crust and his brains have boiled.
The remaining twelve are walking north. Slowly.
Will they reach the border, I asked?
Bah to borders, said sand. Borders are dreams.
Those lines in the sand were drawn by rattlesnakes.

                    But ugh,
            the ergs,
    the eskers,
            the sinks,
    the cirques,
            the barrens,
                    the barchans.
On the crest I needed goggles
as if watching an eclipse,
my boots worn white as cuttlebone
and sand in its cylinders twisting through the sky.

Here we are at last, said sand.
This is *El Gran Desierto del Altar*
where no man has ever set foot.
Even Cortez turned away, Cortez
the killer and his iron army.
And here you stand, pilgrim.

On that crest I thought of Mars
because when sand rubs
            a cinder
it reveals
            a ruby.

But it was a wind from Morocco
put the iron in the face of the sandhills moon,
            so low down
            I looked into it
climbing the north-facing dune,
so low down I looked directly into it
and felt that I could touch the blood bruise on the sky –
that moon the sand had smoked redder than chilli oil.

After that we rested, sand and I,
cool in the corals of Cog
y Brain, a parish that had prospered
under sand's perpetual
curacy, commote of vipers' milk,

every twmpath of Tir y Hwndrwd
a honeyed tomb, a terraced vault.

From there we surveyed the world.
        Sometimes I can be good, said sand.
At Oxyrynchus I blew away from the town
and that is how they discovered the Iliad on a thousand papyri.
        Not all the words, you understand,
that was a poem I needed to rewrite.
But I watched the professors dig for those pages
and wondered when they might realise
        that sand is the true epic.
Because sand is not gossip
        but a gospel
        announcing itself.

        It was there sand told me
its torments. The time it was locked
        in a Palaeolithic vice
and mocked by the scum of the earth;
        when it was confined
        to the empty quarter
        then banished in shame
        to Badiet Esh Sham,
how it must career around the caravans, blind
and unbidden, every door against it:
incontinent sand, the earth's orphan.

Ah, stop whining, sand, I say.
        Take your Ritalin.
        And that's when I look up.

There is ash in my hair, silver in my teeth.
        The children are observing me,
        each with a lunar face;
        and every child an altar, an anvil,
        and every face my own deathmask.

Yes there is my class
   waving their hands with answers
     I can never know.
      Or are they saying goodbye
     as they watch me pass
   grain after grain
  into the hourglass?

La Otra Orilla

1 Tickertape

For days
I never opened my mouth,
afraid of the stranger who would speak with my voice
and the thief who lived under my tongue.

  Learning the language
was like eating its seafood
– *chipirones, pulpitos* –
when Gotan, my friend, took me to the café
and every word was squidgy as a mussel
under its blue door.

  Verbs
were lemon-edged, like samphire;
conjunctions beckoned with their department-store glass:
how I loitered there.

  Then, a breakthrough.
Ice-cream at the *kiosko*,
and a glass of Malbec with Gotan
in a bar made of corrugated iron painted pink;
and that afternoon, waiting for the lights to change on Rivadavia,
I looked up and the sky was full of words.

Immediately
all the bills of lading from La Boca
were blowing like the jacaranda petals around my feet,
and the special offers and the final demands
and the Vallejo stanzas and the bank statements
and Borges's foul copies of *El Aleph*
and every second chapter from *Kiss of the Spider Woman*,
all the molecules of books were adrift on the air.

Next came
the repossessions and the summonses,
the timetables from the language school where Gotan worked,
and soon the languages themselves from the sacristies
of paper, and the professors from the language school
throwing armfuls of idioms out of their office windows,
and the secretaries of the professors from the language school
photocopying their kisses and scattering them from the third storey.

Then the black-browed
subjunctive plummeted like a suicide
and with it the future-perfect, mauve as the magnolia,
and there was Menem's manifesto
and then the biographies of the disappeared
disappearing as the wind hurried them down the *avenidas*
to the sea that would greet them once again.

And with them fell
the love-songs that the student had written for the torturer
so he might serenade his sweetheart on his day off,
and behind them the *empanada* menus
and the words on the cigarette butts
and the bullets and the wine bottles and the toilet walls,
and there were the epitaphs traced from the tombstones
and the paint of the street names scraped off the street signs.

For days
I had not opened my mouth.
I let Gotan do the talking and instead
groaned like my father in his blue smock,

his left cheek fallen, his left arm deciduous, daunted
by the anarchy of his own tongue,
but now, here I was with the soldiers
and the corn-roasters on the Plaza de Mayo
as the words fell upon us in their tickertape blessings.

And in that *pampero* of paper
were words for the desperate and words for the newborn;
there was wealth for the *cartoneros* beyond every dream,
and the beggars around us were filling their trousers with passports
and telephone directories and death sentences,
and there was Gotan lying on the ground
with *La Nación* covering his face
and there I stood with arms outstretched
and the letter 'I' dissolving in my hand
    like a hailstone.

2   *Teatro*

Yes I am coming with golden Colon,
coming to Colonia,
coming with golden Colon
to Colonia across the sea.

    Weekends
I'd go with Gotan to the flea-markets.
There's nothing he loves better
than barter on those San Telmo Sundays
with pimps and astrologers and the admiral
in a uniform mottled like a mirror,
or the country kids come up from the farms
carrying sacks of sunflower seeds.

    Once I found
he'd bought an apparatus that gleamed
like a bordello of glow-worms.
It was an absinthe engine, he whispered,
all spouts and glasses, inlaid with silver

vermiculations. Baudelaire, he said,
is my hero, after DJ Shadow and *mon cher*
Che. Maybe John Coltrane.
And this absintheizer is the crucible
where the senses are rationally,
which means with a recipe, deranged.
Then Gotan grinned like a thief.

We'd seen La Boca's ships scabbed by the sea,
the hulls molten with rust, its lava at their sterns and bows,
and all La Boca's colours in the oil painting
I carried, a few pesos she said, so I paid the artist,
that girl with burgundy about her eyes and vermilion upon her
toenails,
      and carried La Boca through La Boca,
that picture a bargain said Gotan, I am an artist myself you know,
but in soundscapes, recording La Plata's tides,
      my tapeloops in all the clubs,
      the nightclub children in each other's arms
      watching dawn break to my birdsong,
      my remix of the revolution
      with CNN news
      cut to confetti.

      One night we met Gotan
outside an apartment block
where the electricity was turned off
and we could see children's candleshadows
as they went to bed, families ghosting
through winelight.

      Downtown,
Gotan knew the way
and I followed him upstairs to a bar
with a coffee machine so dinted and stained
it might have been some Toledo cuirass
targeted by untold Querandi stones,
and we took our café by the glass
under Teatro Libre's black curtain

and never forget
　　he said
　　　　never forget
the burning palm trees of a bankrupt republic
and that a chief of police will listen forever
to the empire's pornographic sigh.

　　But absinthe, Gotan breathed,
　　　is how the soul communicates.
Its wormwood parables are untold by the tongue.
Drink and you'll discover dreams in the dirt under your fingernails.
Our life must be served in prism sentences.
　　　Abstinence
　　　will be my nemesis.
　　　It's delirium that drives.

Behind the curtain lay a darkness so thick
I could not see my hand
but there was Gotan's hand upon my back
and we sat on school benches
and waited until something
came out of the blackness –
an owl's face
or a woman in owl's feathers –
a woman with a belly white as a garlic
bulb and grinning with her mouth
on fire in an owl's head-dress –
grinning I saw, in front of the drapes
that blacked out even the starlight of my skin.

Hardly the Paradiso, whispered Gotan,
as the torturers explored
pain's tautology. But still
the best seats in the house.

After the show we went for a beer –
the cool Quilmes on our tabletop –
and we drank like men shackled to our cups
until Gotan sat back and sang his nursery rhyme:

from KING DRIFTWOOD (2008)　　　　　　　　　　155

Yes I am coming with golden Colon,
coming to Colonia,
coming with golden Colon
to Colonia across the sea.

And when I wake I will rub
the sleep from my ears
in the house of harpsichords.

But what waited in that darkness?
The regime's rapeocracy.
After the women died
they raped the children
and after the children
they raped the men
and then they raped the dogs
after the men died
before they raped the mossgowned
sloth hung like an angel
in metropolitan amnesia.
And after the women had died
and the children died
they planted rape in this country
and the rapeflower grows in the mountains still
and in the streets. It is pale
     and light
          as lithium,
a herb they say that's medicine
for memory and white as a bride's veil
that drags across the desert dusk
until caught on a cactus.

The next day
I saw Gotan and his girl
with their kettledrums
outside the Casa Rosada;
then later on in all La Boca's bars
kissing the teargas out of each other's eyes.
Haven't we cried enough, the girl asked,

aren't there enough tears in this world?
Damn them, damn them, she waved,
as if the generals stooped about them now like vultures in gold braid.

Yes, think of Colonia,
where cats curl up on cannonballs
and breakfast lasts all day
until sleep, il generalissimo,
drafts you to a dream.

And when I wake I will wake
where I always wake
in the house of harpsichords.

The answer, said Gotan, is anarchy.
That's why I will never buy an apartment in Puerto Madryn
or watch Tom Cruise at the multiplex
or accept a PIN number from HSBC.
        As to the bankers,
        stuff their hearts with pepper
        and their bellies with broken glass.
        Freeze them in prisons of Patagonian ice.

And soon he was whistling the march to the scaffold
that Berlioz wrote, and laughing like
Berlioz's absinthe-coloured demons
as if they were dancing out of the metro
and dragging the souls of soldiers and blackgloved
police and sneaks and senators and helicopter
pilots, of pimps, of *putas* and poets,
of pacifiers and expurgating editors,
the fat, the fascistic, the freighted with lies,

the disinformers, the unmakers, the antipriests
and antiteachers, the lawyers
bound like *burros* to each other by their Jaeger ties,
the journalists who had never interrogated themselves,
dragging them through the turnstile
past the painted aborigines

who once walked naked on the glaciers,
past the prehistoric bones of flightless birds,
past conquistadors who watched from their battlements
immortal in the twilight armour of armadillos:
> to the train to hell or Ushuaia,
> whichever station comes first.

3 *Las Cataratas*

It is time to leave
but Gotan will not let us
go. One last adventure, he pleads,
to make sense of everything.

Forgetting the city we take the Marco Polo north
and travel all night and the only sign of human life
is firelight struck in oil drums
and bodies prone around each dying blaze.

But what arrives with the dark
is lightning. Gotan says he is a connoisseur
of lightning; it is masque and muse
to him, an electric mass.
Tonight its incendiaries race out of a sky
the colour of a tattooist's inks.

My seat is next to the coffee machine.
The Marco Polo coffee is black and hot and so sweet
I shiver at the first taste, trembling
with the saccharine rush. But now I hold my cup
in both hands as if refusing to let go
while the land dries out, the forests change,
the pampas stars burn huge and indecipherable
and gauchos ride with us a moment
out of the mist. And I hear Gotan
singing in his sleep

Iguaçu night
Iguaçu night
pumas black as pumice
in the Iguaçu night.

Soon we are the only ones left.
As we alight the bus is driven away.
Or perhaps it simply disappears.

Over there, says Gotan, and we have to follow.
At last, he says. Here are *las cataratas*.
At our feet a pit opens.
Inside the pit a rainbow writhes.
Here there is sky where there should be earth.
Here there are birds where they might be fish.

    Only swifts invade
    this void but
    Gotan says the pit
    is not for us.

Who comes with us? we call.
No one, says Gotan. We are the last
    but for those toucans –
    those toucans with their terrible beaks,
    their stone language;
    those toucans with telephones in their mouths –
    those toucans can too.

And Gotan sings to us

    Rainforest night
    rainforest night
    pumas black as pumice
    in the rainforest night.

At our feet
the pit of white light
where we will be unearthed.

We can go no further —
no further than the ledge where the swifts lodge
in their black moss, mollusc-birds with wings
sharp as mosque-moons, the last creatures
of all before the world ends
and the rainbow makes a bridge
through the abyss,
a bridge that we must
trust.

You should understand, says Gotan, this is the only way.
Behind us is the *tigre* that took the park ranger's son.
Its eyes are *aguardiente*, each paw a lily pad.

There is no bridge, we tell him.
Che baludo, don't leave us on the edge of nothing.
    At our feet
    a pit of white light
    where we will be unearthed.

Jump, says Gotan. Behind us is the *tigre*
that murdered Maradona's mother. One last adventure,
my friends, think of all we have been through together:
    think of the toucans —
    those toucans with their terrible beaks,
    their stone language;
    those toucans with telephones in their mouths.
    The *tigre* took those toucans too.

At our feet the pit opens;
inside the pit a rainbow writhes.
It is more than time, says Gotan.
The clocks have started to go backwards.
We must join *los desaparecidos*
and then this last adventure will make sense of everything.
Behind us is the *tigre* the Guarani trapped
that Evita might wrap her shoulders in its silks.
To understand our history we must cross the bridge.

So I take the step.
I take the step and the coffee
is black and hot and so sweet I tremble as I taste.
And there is Gotan, his head against my head,
whispering in his sleep

Iguaçu night
Iguaçu night
pumas black as pumice
in the Iguaçu night

And there are the herds and there the stars' junta,
for still there are more stars than steers,
and as we gaze together at the roots of the day
the meniscus of the new moon
is pale as a palmito
above us this night, this noon
where we must be unearthed.

Eavesdropping

4 a.m.
and the swifts
over the house in the disappearing
dark, the swifts open-mouthed, ten,
twenty of them, thirty swifts now
and in every open-mouthed swift I picture
a heart the size of a hawthorn berry,
blood red to bursting those swift hearts,
thirty hearts in thirty swifts
over the house this morning where I stand
naked at the window, listening to my own heart –
perhaps the closest I will get to prayer –
and eavesdropping on the silence of the morning
where every swift is a black new moon upon the black mosque of
the air.

The Castaway

Sleepless
I keep sleep in my pocket,
insomnia a sea-urchin language
and the nights strung together dried like chillies,
the red, the black, the ceaseless, the unbearable,
the darkness of chilli wombs rattling with stars.

But every night
a whale in the bay
spits at the moon.
Though it does not exist
how quickly I put my serenade together
for our low-tide rendezvous.

Look at me, I say to the no one there.
One day these bones will be silver in the sea holly.
But today I darken, I darken,
my skin a caste-marked congregation in a chancel of salt.

The town astronomers
are camped upon the dune
measuring Mars as it rides over Somerset.
Maybe I should throw my spear at them
or serve rainwater in an oystershell.

Such a current.
I call it *El Generalissimo* –
for only the current can say
where the disappeared people have gone.

I fear lightning, jellyfish, the uncomprehending mind, call
centres, ticks, the data protection act, search parties, autopsy, sand-
fleas, journalism, tourists, tiger sharks, whirlpools, translation,
the storm ten miles offshore whose ziggurat is built from one
billion tons of rain, rain bricks, imperial staterooms of rain with
rain's imperial family now waving from their balcony overhead.

It was for this I bartered
my breath? But at dawn a footprint,
and in twilight a crab army
circumnavigates the camp.
    Meanwhile I'm refining
my religion.
        To hell
with the sutras of sand:
every day that gospel changes.
My latest god is the driftwood god and I am driftwood's dizziest
                                                    disciple.
See his altars with their pilot lights ablaze upon the tide.

My mermaid I made of marram
the storm stole, she lifted, green
grass angel, over the point,
not an outline left of her or a
trace of the garden I trod her in the chalk,
and after weeks waiting not a word to her
guardian of the one who ascended
without sin or sign, my
wife from the midden,
my wife in mid
air.

The cormorant is always
black. But not blacker
than the blacknesses the ocean will become:
even the cormorant's eye will be black that an hour ago
was the Peruvian gold of Mars as it scorched the sky.

    Destiny, they say,
is all: our pre-natal
navigation. So the poet sets out
over the shelves of Spezia
and there's my mother madcap on the shore
sewing his shipwreck into a shroud.

from KING DRIFTWOOD (2008)   163

Every day
the sea smells stronger on my skin.
At last I am utterly clean,
anointed with crowfeathers, battery
acid, the fair's cinnamon
doughnuts, sulphur in the dune-rift
and fire from the fumaroles in the seabed,
until my blood rings against salt's armour.

So, which sea tonight?
The waif?
The wolf?
Yes.

Traeth yr Afon low tide:
the beach a looted exchequer:
barbarians streaming away.
I start again.

Now the current is dark and all its candles
pinched, its voices vanished like so many
voices that failed at midnight, and the sea's library
in darkness, in its greatest darkness, every book of it
and every page fused to blackness, every word and signature
translated into the language of the dark.

Patience he played
and patience he showed.
I'll show him patience, that no one there.
Here's the wayfarer tree upon the shore –
as if my father had left his diamonds and spades
all over the beach.

August
I'm spending under a hunter's moon.
Tides come in like brickdust,
and all the sprockled moths mad in the wall rocket.
Sometimes I lie on the seabed
to look at the sun.

And sometimes I think drowning's
    a white door
    behind a white
    door where a fire
    burns on a dark
      isthmus.

First
there is an island
    then
there is no island
    then
there is.

    Or:
a sleeper in the ocean
who rises and
        shakes himself
out of his limestone trance
        every eleven hours.

    In my own dream
      I was a glass
statue on the sand with the sea
surreptitious behind the mist.
      And in my glass belly
beat the last
    Adonis of the dunes,
the last thought I would ever have,
      the last creature I could dare to be.
      I stood,
a statue on a shell-dust plinth,
the invisible ocean's foam
to my femurs and the butterfly
tormented in the glass web
      of my veins.

    They told me not to swim
at night, but the cormorant is a great cartographer

and I follow the compass in his heart.
       Yet who knows these roads like me?
I put out my hand and the darkness pulls me in
and I join the army of the invisibles
whose breath is black, whose blood is black
and whose wine is the colour of the waters under the waters.
                 They are waiting for me
                 in the amnesiac room:
they are waiting for me to open my black mouth
and tell them all I have learned of the collision of midnights,
of the sea's unseen catastrophes.

       My sentry
is the mullein in its greatcoat.
And strange – the sea going out and going
out and going beyond me somehow,
so in place of the garden where I floated
– nose and ears stoppered by the wave's pollen –
lie the bureaucracies of mud
       and a conger family
       fletched like school railings.

Television people come to ask
what I eat. Only oysters
oiled with samphire, I say:
or fennel's green shuttlecocks;
maybe kedgeree of seabass seared on a basket of kale.
(More truthfully scroungings from the wheelie at the Seagull
                                              Room.)
Now I'm planning my own series after the soaps.

But the current insists.
       Over the shoulder of the world it comes.
       And I who was sealed
       am a honeycomb.

A long way out.
             Oh never so far.
Over my head the butterfly is moving

away from the citadel and its arcades.
     Not that way, I want to shout,
that way is twenty miles without an orchid mouth.
But there it goes, as if it knew what I do not –
     black through my squint
and trembling
     like a sunspot.

Yes, I bartered my breath
for this. Here the sea's anaerobic
clerks tend their screens, every
molecule awarded its place,
never ending their trials at the terminals.

Now the sea drinks with me, bringing cup after cup.
What a night we have together, rolling in one another's arms,
and drowning's the second
impermissible dream. Each wave is a flume
and a fugue, high pressure August swell lifting me light
as the whipweed till each wave is a fog of dirty gold
where the swimmers are smiling with their cuttle teeth and then
                       each wave
a child at my ankle and then a mother to my mouth,
for her salt milk will make me strong as starfish,
as dead men's ropes, and I'm a belly bursting like a hot
                    Dominican plum.
Here's the wine I wanted most and never was allowed.

The Saint of Tusker Rock

1

I served the surf.
I suffered it.

A saviour, I thought,
a form in the foam,

some message that was
mine and meant for me.

What arrived was a ship
whose men spoke like gulls,

not bothered about gods, only the eel
they saw in my smokery,

a conger black and
gold and grinning on its
gallows. Strong meat,

but in their firelight we were
souls together sharing

a cup, safe for a night
and sure, at least, of that.

So many strangers but I remember them all.
Broken by thirst they would stagger ashore
to my freshwater spring. When they had drunk
and fallen asleep I could look into their faces
        and see their dreams.
So why was it then I never thought my own well could run dry?

Apprentice to salt,
I come from a vanished church.
While I swim my sackcloth swings on seakale;
a leathery man, you'd say, his mouth the imperial
purple of the whinberry.

Yes
they tell stories about
a castaway naked on the rock
waving the driftwood between his legs –
that old goat's greeting to his god.

A child lives with me.
No novice, she has ten summers and eleven winters
and was picking damsons in the dunes
when she saw the wolves in single file come through Cwm y Gaer,
the pack nose to tail,
one's paws perfect in the pawprints of the next,
their pelts of limestone, of seawater.
For a while she stayed with me, blithe and bonny,
my little belter who speaks the old language,
her breasts hard as fennel bulbs,
whispering like sand into my ear
her words for darkness, her barbarous words for prayer.

3

Everything you have I foresaw:
my mirror is the mother-of-pearl's mist upon the palm.

That's how I watched Stonehenge go by
on its rafts, the bluestones coming
out of the west, lashed with hemp.
And maybe they waved –
those oyster-eaters, those temple sailors –
and began to dream of Babylon.

Later, I sat in the Plaza for the first night
of *Silence of the Lambs*.
Anthony Hopkins was our local boy
made good, but half-way through
I noticed his eyes were
dead. And I realised
that where there is no god
man must pray to a stone.

4

Now outside in Llewellyn Street
sulphur slurs the air
and slovens sleep through Sundays.
Whether we wake or not
Silurians ever ever ever
shall be slaves.

So who will be our Spartacus?
                    It is getting late.
But I smile when I think of Kirk Douglas
with the star-shaped dimple in his chin
like a bullet hole or a cleaned-out cancer cut.
I heard him roar in the Plaza's thrilling dark
but cannot remember now if he was crucified or not.

5

In the bay
I swam beside a basking shark
and in its eye
glimpsed the first day of this world.
It too is praise
of paradise.

But should I ever trust the sea?
Every day a different bride:
the oyster-thief, the samphire
turning red,
        the surfer who is
a ghost on the slipway,
exquisite through mist
his contemplation of these waters.
But that whisper of delirium,
right, left, above my head?
Ah, the goldfinches
in the grykes, in the black
arms of the bittersweet,
in limestone's menagerie
of extinctions. Yes, the goldfinches
of the cliff top, gone like courtesans
gossiping to bed.

Now at dawn I look from
my attic. Well, here's a cold
crucifixion. The night's tide
has brought the jellyfish in.
There lies one, snake
in a wine glass, the foetus
of a stone. But something molten
lingering at its crater, and in the void
where the heart should be, and about its
outflung arms. Such
an experiment of being
that the sea delivers to my feet.
And who but I to greet our visitor,
this thalidomide child upon
the sand, a broken carafe
the wave sweeps away.

6

After years of gardening here's what I recall:
to thrive the soul needs a south-facing wall.

I made this home
where the earth ends
— a bivouac beside St John's —
and watched it fill with red beanflowers that the bees love,
red as the bees themselves.

The rain barrels were brimful in the Baptist's garden
which once was my chosen church.
I can stand by the beans I planted and see
in this pod's white pith a pulpit
where a furious fruit is announced.

Then Monday night bell practice starts simple
but soon the changes challenge my own rhythms
as the bells are opening and closing
like the Baptist's marigolds in the dusk,
time racing until it's dawn-dusk in seconds,
daylight for a moment and then the dark again
and the bells' vines vanishing under my skin
and the bells' perfume soaking my skin
like the iron-coloured gooseberries waiting in wine.

7

On the highest ridge
I pricked my girl child's skin
with the tattoo of a blue hare.
And ordained:
she shall be swift:
she shall lie open-eyed under the moon:
she shall not linger long in her whirlpool of grass.

These days I walk the coast alone
and feel my mind skip like a stone —

the grey, the green, the amethyst
of the rock pool's eucharist.

Yip, there's a thousand tracks on that iPod
and every one the word of God.

So too is there life in a lightless wood.
Look at the honeysuckle's circuitry:
it spirals out of the earth and shows where the power will travel
        and how it will move.
Soon there's a canopy where the leaves will press
in passover and a buzzard at roost on that reef of leaves
        never knowing I stand below
            and see into the hurricane of its eye.

8

But mine is the vanished church.
My cathedral? A quiver of sticks.
        I took it down,
        laid it low
        in the sandy tilth,
the roof beam, the spandrels, the flying buttresses
where at the last hung only ivy of sea-mist.

While the garden filled with fruits
the beansticks were a belfry of bees.
But that pyramid now is a pyre beside St John's,
and the bells' music a lorrypark throb
or a rain of horseshoes or oranges or broken black umbrellas,
each bell an engine of ecstasy its bellman would say,
though I think the bells are chess played in the sky,
or mathematics, which always had a mosquito sound for me,
but now is bellmetal in this bellyard.

9

I watched my child place a seed in the ground.
Only we knew the place and only we knew the secret.

We watered it.
Something started to grow.
Who would believe a stone when a leaf astonishes?

First day:
dew's duty done:
rust already on the rose.

Second day:
the infinitesimals
building.

Third day:
look aside once and your software is out of date.
Nothing stops now.

Fourth day:
breathe the avalanche: grass is speeded up:
this is what a miracle means.

Fifth day:
locusts. We're refugees
upon the highways of the leaf.

Sixth day:
harvest. While the world's computers
write a new gospel.

Seventh day:
in darkness we bury ourselves without blessing –
who waited too long for our lives to begin.

Why do they play the organ?
Ponderous and sinister,
    it's a thin soul's thunder.
    A fugitive from its fugues
I find a corner of the bar where I sit with my latest love
    – the necromancer, Madam X –
who sports black nails and a surfeit of nerves
and all her suitors' names inked around her nipples:
    dav gav moz maz
    cynwyd cewydd cornelius colman
    poor tudwg whose chancel has filled with bats
    and Dewi who vanished in a sandstorm.
All sweetwater saints who slept under sallow,
saltwater souls who sailed to the whirlpool.

But the tattoos on this woman are laborious as a suicide note.
Did no one tell her there are words that cannot be written down?
    Yet if vodka and orange make her feel alive
    there must be a miracle in the mix.
That's what the landlord says as he hands us the DVD control
to his Monday afternoon movie –
The Great Escape, of course.
Our favourite part is where Steve McQueen
is caught in the barbed wire
and we zoom in on how he is pinned to the earth
by the totalitarian thorns.

    Oh yes, I think.
    And grin.

And so the aeons pass
    as we allow them to pass
    on the peninsula.

This afternoon I find an albatross.
Wounded it has wandered
to lie wide as a windmill
on the tump of Twmpath Tom Brython.
As I look into the well
of its woebegone eye
I see what our sailors never saw –
the shoals dispersed, the icebergs
a paper chain upon a school window.

How she has grown, my wolf-wary child:
she needs no costume now
who is both chooser and chosen,
adding her own milk
to the wave, this shiggly
girl with arms across breasts
which are as white as wheatears,
her habit the surrounding surf,
the salt itself her psalter.

She will betray me I know like all the rest but still I comb her
hair and it is silver down to the root paler even than the stud in
the petal of her ear while her dress is the blue check with that
elderberry stain on the sleeve that won't wash out and she is
such a madam walking always one yard behind on the road to
school past the video shop with all last night's cartridges pushed
through the door and the hairdresser's where already a woman
is bent double with damp strands over her face and although we
hurry we are always late so I give her the money and the white
plastic inhaler and then I am back on Rhych Avenue with the
sea's breath on my neck.

From behind the wall
I watch the scourgers scour the grass:
boys with sticks
come to thump the pumpkin like a big bass drum.

There is nothing so glorious as that gourd,
joined to the earth by its artery,
served at night by a gardener
who has slept there with his thermos.
But as the pumpkin swelled
it grew too huge to hide.

So the children found it.
They touched its skin,
strange as phosphorus.

Amazed
they stroked it
like a breast.

One child corkscrewed out a piece
and tasted it.

Spat out that bread.
Pissed his poisons over it.

Then they stove it with sticks,
wrenched it from the vine,
its eggmeat whitegold as a wedding ring
broken by their boots.

Last they stoned it like a saint,
that new loaf, that god-gourd
grown beyond concealment
but trespassing in someone else's creation.

Now
black snow.
Black kiss
of the eclipse.
  In the garden I stand
before dawn. The black hour. All is gaunt
and ghosted. Ice in the barrel
sighs like a man asleep,
a man who might never wake;
as if sleep is now the silicon in his bones
and the carbon in his heart.
    But such is ice, the foetus
that floats in the ultrascan:
an isthmus in the ocean of its mother.
Now the earth I have dug through the centuries is frozen against me.
    I have come home to a locked house.

Starving, I smash a pane and roust out
a root of horseradish from its holt,
and suck it, earth and all, the sand on it my sugarcane,
bite it, gnaw it, make it my medicine.
To the manna born I am this morning,
its medulla hotting my mouth,
hotter than the host in his wafer
or mead mulled and pokered in a picket fire.
This horseradish loves the soil I sieve and the sand that suckles it.
Where all was barren it is a staff stiff as a burin,
the horseradish that grows in my plot
   – iron cotter pin, dirty sceptre –
    and keeps a beggar warm.

Through a waste of winters here's what I recall:
to thrive the soul needs a south-facing wall.

Ages ago
this was a market:
horseradish leaves like flutings of green enamel,
crab apples, salt cod, coneyskins, mussel shells,
remedies for gutrot and the clap,
and the language changing colour
like the stained glass above the chancel in St John's,
cargoes of the tongue unhitched where the sailors caulk the boats,
the pitch blacking the children's clothes.
You will never get it off,
the sailors said,
no matter how hard you rub.

I have traced my ancestry back four thousand years
to a family who stood on the ridge
and could feel the storm before they saw it:
their sky an owl's
egg
starting to
crack.

Now from this crest the whirlwind
seems a black enamel lighthouse
rising out of the water
with the sun a prisoner within it:
so pale and jittery,
that dying king.

To comfort myself in such weather
I remember that on reaching fifty
Phil Everly gave Don Everly a pound of gold.

Here in the laburnum I count sixteen goldcrests,
imagine sixteen goldcrest hearts,
hear sixteen goldcrest songs.

I listen to the Everly Brothers,
I listen to the goldcrest songs,
but Don Everly does not hang upside down in my laburnum tree.

16

On Judgement Day
I will stand before
a tribunal of trilobites
and justify my life.
Here's what I will say:

Parched, I became what I feared most:
a dry man
stooped to a pool.
But those who pray to salt must pay in thirst.

I drank and went mad
and this is what I learned.
There's a kind of life that scuffles
in the scurvygrass. We are not that.

A walker and a winterer,
I never seek but sense the nerve and sinew of the sea.
But must finish where I begin
   – tracing a newel of sandstone
through a greyer level, following a staircase
into the strata to where the change is made:
      different codings,
coolings; whose rocks are fractious children
and the glacier carries centuries in its snout.

I am fallen like the forest in its fanfare of fern fire,
      but always the red

against the grey,
their atoms in attrition, the scars and sutures
    where an empire ended.

    The seas rose
and flames poured from the wound in the side of the world.
    I drank and went mad
and came eye to eye with myself in the rock.
Because there's no sane man would ever think
    we are what a fossil dreams.

Now sunfish run the tides.
Warmer, warming this shore.
Even here they find their way
– their brass to bless.

Consider the cocklegirl
with her waxpaper cones;
the coins in her satchel, the bite on her neck.
I booked two places on the Skymaster
but she laughed at an old man's whiskery ears.

And I who was bright as the chiton in its mail
must cling to a precipice.

17

Limping along Cwm Befos
I see the winter oak with a fox in its arms
    while beyond is Exmoor
    electric, dark as dulse,
the sunlight leaning like timber in a joiner's yard,
    the shafts
        the spars
    the sweetsawn
        sprucedust
    scattered on the air.

Beyond me the storm is standing out of the sea,
a black bolster whose blade divides the water from the land.
        But already I am leaving,
I who planned the node and name for anemone and nematode
        already I have started
to disappear.

        And suddenly I see
that the scourgers have tied Christ's
legs. They are beating him with nettles
and the dust of the violet nettleflowers
is settling as a garden at his feet
and the Renaissance is growing out of it
while behind the New Emerald Chinese takeaway
the badlands are awaiting us.
        But step inside:
you'll know mullein's yellow millions
and find fennel's first green to final gold.

18

Behind me Exmoor
    with centuries
    with centuries

the cocklegirl floating through the dusk
        bearing her tray,
her blue bandanna with the stars upon it,
the moon and sun that govern our griefs.

In the gwter lies galena in a teagreen tier,
the caverns, the cairns, the choruses in coral weed.
This kind of life a walker wears and a winterer weathers.

  Look. There it is:
  the tornado
  like a test tube
  filled with blood.

Even those who have spent millennia in the rock
will have their rousting out.
We are not that.

I drank and went mad —
a saint in the splash zone
haloed with rocksalt.
Now here I am with my thirst beside me,
the last companion.

Yet three glow worms shine in the High Tide Arcade:
the magi's journey has brought them far across the dunes
and into the fair.
      What else can they take from us but
       a mouthful of candyfloss,
          our driftwood cross,
                    tickets for the Haunted House?

While beneath the Megablitz
in the terrible tongue
the cocklegirl is counting backwards towards the black zero.
After all I've done for her that's how I'm repaid.

         We will vanish together
but each must find his own way out,
must never seek but sense the nerve and sinew of the sea:
          all weathers to wander
          the forbidden places,
          this kind of life
          this kind of life,
          the last of a kind.

Or so says a madman
who forgot his own name.

The Fox in the National Museum of Wales

He scans the frames but doesn't stop,
the fox who has come to the museum today,
his eye in the Renaissance
and his brush in the Baroque.

Between dynasties his footprints
have still to fade, between the Shan and the Yung,
the porcelain atoms shivering at his touch,
ah, lighter than the emperor's breath, drinking rice wine from the
                                                                  bowl,

daintier than the eunuch pouring wine.

I came as quickly as I could
but already the fox had left the Industrial Revolution behind,
his eye has swept the age of atoms,
the Taj Mahal within the molecule.

The fox is in the fossils and the folios, I cry.
The fox is in Photography and the Folk Studies Department.
The fox is in the flux of the foyer,
the fox is in the flock,
the fox is in the flock.

Now the fox sniffs at the dodo
and at the door of Celtic orthography.
The grave-goods, the chariots, the gods of darkness,
he has made their acquaintance on previous occasions.

There, beneath the leatherbacked turtle he goes,
the turtle black as an oildrum,
under the skeleton of the whale he skedaddles,
the whalebone silver as bubblewrap.

Through the light of Provence moves the fox, through
the Ordovician era and the Sumerian summer,
greyblue the blush on him, this one who has seen so much,

blood on the bristles of his mouth,
and on his suit of iron filings the air fans like silk.

Through the Cubists and the Surrealists
this fox shimmies surreptitiously,
past the artist who has sawn himself in half
under the formaldehyde sky
goes this fox shiny as a silver
fax in his fox coat,
for at a foxtrot travels this fox
backwards and forwards in the museum.

Under the bells of *Brugmansia*
that lull the Ecuadoran botanists to sleep,
over the grey moss of Iceland
further and further goes this fox,
passing the lambs at the feet of Jesus,
through the tear in Dante's cloak.

How long have I legged it
after his legerdemain, this fox
in the labyrinth, this fox that never hurries
yet passes an age in a footfall, this fox
from the forest of the portrait gallery
to Engineering's cornfield sigh?

I will tell you this.
He is something to follow,
this red fellow.
This fox I foster –
he is the future.

No one else
has seen him yet.
But they are closing
the iron doors.

Index of Titles and First Lines

Titles are in italic, first lines in roman.

INDEX OF TITLES AND FIRST LINES